BY PETER CRILLY

Sport Media
A Trinity Mirror Business

ACKNOWLEDGEMENTS

I would like to thank my wife Faye for putting up with me for the past 21 years and my two beautiful daughters (Jenna and Natalie) for their support. Of course a big thank you to my family and friends for being there, and to Ron Richards and Bill Bygroves and all at 'the Bridge' for their support. Other mentions must go to Stephen Done from the Liverpool FC Museum & Tour Centre for his help and guidance; Colin Wright and Michael Yip for the use of their photographs; Kingsley Gratick and Ben Terrett at The Design Conspiracy; and all at Trinity Mirror Sport Media, especially Ken Rogers for his vision and belief and James Cleary and Barry Parker for their hard work. But most of all to you the fans, for buying this book and making it all worthwhile.

Published in Great Britain in 2007 & 2008 by:

Trinity Mirror Sport Media,

PO Box 48, Old Hall Street,

Liverpool L69 3EB

Executive Editor: KEN ROGERS

Art Editor: RICK COOKE

Designer: BARRY PARKER

Editorial Assistant: JAMES CLEARY

ISBN 978-1905-26622-7 : Printed and finished by Brolink

INTRODUCTION

From humble beginnings back in 1892, Liverpool Football Club has come a long way - and seen an awful lot of changes. As all Liverpool fans know, if you want to know about Anfield there are books; if you want to know about players and managers or even the Kop and the fans, it's been done before. Even if you want to know about Liverpool in Europe or other cup competitions it's been done - even statistics and figures. It's all out there by players, managers (past and present) and fans alike.
So what's new? What can I tell you that is not already out there for you to read? What will this book tell you that you may not already know?
Well what about the kits that made us what we are today. The years that we wore them (and in some cases why we wore them), the kits that proved lucky and the ones that were not so lucky.
I came across the idea when I was trying to collect as many kits from our history as I could find. I decided to do some research and found some great information for a book so as to make it easier to follow and appreciate for like-minded fans.

To make it more interesting and relevant I decided to add other aspects to it. For each time period I have considered players associated with a particular kit, who was in charge, the on and off-field tales and a special 'Did You Know?' section.
Often overlooked are other aspects, such as the changing face of the kit, badges and logos, numbers and other noticeables from a certain period or season.
Split into sections including either one season or more, the book takes into account the number of kit changes made and resultedly, we have split the book accordingly, taking in as many kits as possible from the club's 116-year history. As an extra bonus, there's a 'Miscellaneous' section including kit ads, training tops and one or two other surprises!
Where possible I have attempted to be as accurate as I could, although discrepencies may occur but where there is uncertainty, I have aimed to state that doubt.
This is for the best football fans in the world. I hope you enjoy it.
PETER S. CRILLY

CONTENTS

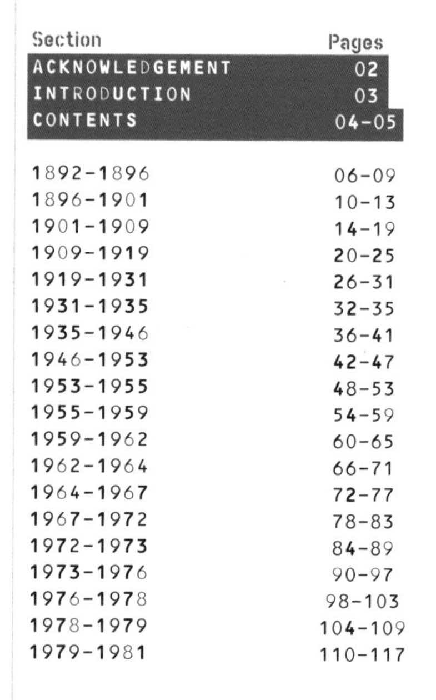

HITACHI
HITACHI

1892-1896

Mac men, pioneers in blue and white

1892-1896

92/96 PLAYERS Malcolm McVean, Matt McQueen
MANAGER John McKenna

ABOUT THE KIT

From their formation in 1892 up to the end of the 1895-96 season, Liverpool never wore the red kit for which they are now world famous. The actual kit was blue, white and black. The shirt was blue and white halves (similar to Blackburn Rovers' current strip, although quarters have also been suggested) with a button collar. The shorts were black (or white) knee-length trousers with possibly black (or blue) socks and white sock tops. The away shirt was a white-buttoned shirt similar in style to the home version while the bottom of the garment was sewn up so you would pull the shirt on. The shorts and socks were the same as the ones used for the home strip.

FAMOUS MATCH

Liverpool 7-1 Rotherham T. (Friendly).

Two days before their Lancashire League debut, the Reds met Rotherham Town on September 1st, 1892 - their first-ever match. A.W. Kelvin (2), Malcolm McVean (who holds the honour of being the first player to score for the club in league football), Tom Wyllie (2) and John Miller were the scorers, with an untraced player also on target.

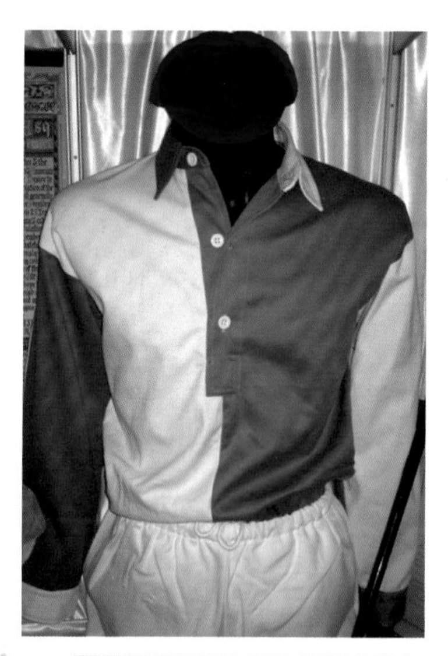

LFC Museum replica 1892

ON-FIELD

Beginning life in the Lancashire League, Liverpool's `team of Macs' claimed the title and a Lancashire Senior Cup double in their first season. Despite an inferior goal difference to second-placed Blackpool, they were deemed champions on goal average.

As a result, they were successfully elected to the Football League, beginning life in the Second Division. With average crowds trebling, the Reds romped to a second successive title, remaining unbeaten and winning every home game as they secured promotion to the top flight. Unfortunately, the success was too good to be true and Liverpool found the First Division a step too far, finishing bottom of the 16-team First Division - although they would soon bounce back, winning the Second Division in 1895-96.

Despite three first places in four years, the FA Cup brought little cheer, a run to the third round (the Reds started in round one) being their best effort in 1893-94.

Away 1893

Liverpool v. Newtown 1892

Match sketch 1892

OFF-FIELD

The away top was actually used as a spare home shirt, as it was the home team's responsibility to change to their `whites' if the opposing team's colours clashed with your own. This rule was issued in 1891.

DID YOU KNOW?

The Lancashire Senior Cup final of 1893 saw the `Reds' beat Everton 1-0. The match was sponsored...by Bovril. John Houlding tried to keep the name `Everton'.

On February 18th, 1896, Liverpool beat Rotherham Town 10-1.

In 1895-96, the Reds set the record for goals scored in the Second Division (106).

1896-1901

Title first for Mac men

1896-1901

96/01 PLAYERS Thomas Bradshaw, Alex Raisbeck
MANAGER Tom Watson

ABOUT THE KIT

Research by Liverpool FC statistician Eric Doig uncovered the first official game when the club wore red. On September 1st, 1896 (the opening day of the new season in Division One), Liverpool defeated The Wednesday 2-1 at Olive Grove courtesy of two goals by George Allan. Local newspaper reports claimed the team wore red shirts and white pants. Our image on the opposite page also confirms the change, the sketch being from November 1896.
The new shirt incorporated a dark red or black stand collar with buttons down the front. The shorts were white, knee length with the socks black. The away version was the same, but with white shirt and shorts (and black socks).

Away 1897-99

DID YOU KNOW?

Liverpool's match against Blackburn Rovers in September, 1896, which finished 1-0 to the Ewood Park side, saw six goals disallowed.
Thomas Bradshaw became the club's first England international, playing against Ireland in February 1897.

FAMOUS MATCH

West Brom 0-1 Liverpool (Division One).

The victory at rock-bottom Albion secured Liverpool's first-ever First Division title. The Reds went into the game behind Sunderland on goal difference, but a late John Walker goal sealed it.

ON-FIELD

After securing First Division status in 1896 after only one season in the second tier, Liverpool began to establish themselves as one of the leading sides in the country. Subsequent finishes of 5th, 9th, 2nd and 10th hinted at potential success, before glory at last in 1901. Two years previous Aston Villa pipped the Reds by two points (although their 5-0 defeat of the Reds on the final day suggest they were worthy champions). This time it was Liverpool who overhauled the leaders with a victory in their last game at West Brom, when a draw would have been good enough. Ironically it was Sunderland who were second, the team who Reds boss Tom Watson had previously led to three Championships. Indeed, it was a 1-0 defeat of the Wearsiders that sparked off a 12-match unbeaten run which went a long way to securing the success.
A first-ever FA Cup semi-final appearance was also achieved in 1897, the Reds losing 3-0 to eventual Double-winners Aston Villa.

1896

OFF-FIELD

John Walker's title-clinching goal meant that the inside-forward had won an English League winners' medal to go with the Scottish equivalent he secured with previous side Hearts.

Thomas Bradshaw

1901-1909

Reds Kop the Second, then the First...

1901-1909

01/09 PLAYERS Sam Raybould, Jack Parkinson
MANAGER Tom Watson

ABOUT THE KIT

The onset of the 1901-02 season saw the introduction of a new red shirt. Consisting of ribbed material, the collar was mandarin with a single button-through placket, through which a lace could be worn. The shorts were white 'baggies' (known as knickerbockers) and the socks were red.
The away strip was predominantly white with a red collar and shoulder area. The collar was mandarin with lace and red cuffs with pure white baggie shorts, and black socks. Incidentally by the time of the 1907-08 season, black socks were used for both the home and away kits and incorporated two white bands across the tops. Incidentally, it is around this period when some players are pictured in striped shirts, with white being one of the colours. However, we uncovered no evidence to suggest that such kits were ever worn by Liverpool.

1908 Cartoon

Home 1900s

ON-FIELD

Back-to-back titles of Division Two in 1905 and the First Division in 1906 stand out as major high points during this eight-year period. From the lows of relegation in 1903-04 (just three years after taking their first First Division crown), the club bounced straight back, winning the Second Division. The following 1905-06 season did not suggest anything but struggle after Liverpool lost their first three games (winning only three of the first eight) but a subsequent run of 19 points from a possible 20 (two points for a win) cemented an unlikely challenge. The goals of Joe Hewitt (24) and the emergence of goalkeeper Sam Hardy saw the Reds become the first side to win Division Two and Division One in successive seasons. They would finish four points ahead of Preston. That season also saw the club come close to a first League and FA Cup Double, reaching the 1906 Cup semi-final. It would be Everton who denied them a final against Newcastle United though, winning 2-0 at Villa Park and eventually taking the trophy to secure a Merseyside double. There was to be more silverware, as the final game saw Liverpool beat Corinthians 5-1 to take the Sheriff of London Charity Shield - a forerunner to the current FA Community Shield.

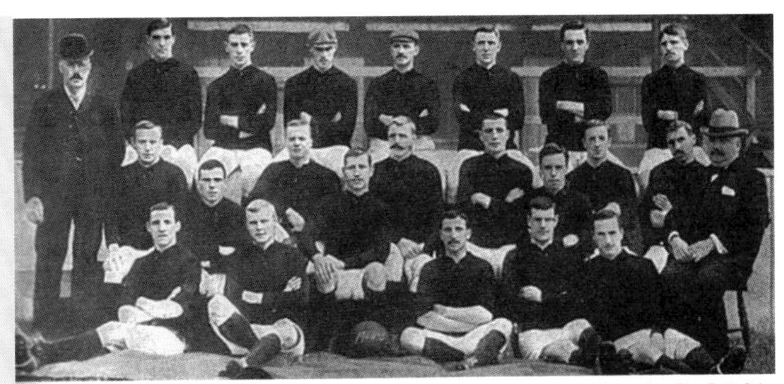

Liverpool, Second Division champions, pictured in 1904-05. Back row (left to right): Maurice Parry, David Murray, Peter Platt, Teddy Doig, Billy Dunlop, Charlie Wilson, C.Evans. Middle row: W.Connell (trainer), George Fleming, James Hughes, John Carlin, Tom Chorlton, Jack Cox, George Lathom, Alex Raisbeck, Tom Watson (secretary). On ground: Arthur Goddard, Robert Robinson, Sam Raybould, Richard Morris, Joe Hewitt, Jack Parkinson, James Garside.

1904-05

OFF-FIELD

The club's founder John Houlding died on 17th March, 1902 aged 69.

FAMOUS MATCH

Liverpool 9-2 Grimsby Town (Division One).

SQUAD LINE-UP 07-08

Some of the Liverpool team and officials from 1907-08 - with a lace collar seemingly optional on some of the players.

DID YOU KNOW?

Sam Raybould set a club record of **31** goals in **33** games in the 1902-03 season.
Liverpool were the first team to win the Second Division and First Division titles back-to-back.
The original Kop was built in 1906. It was named the 'Spion Kop' by *Liverpool Daily Post & Echo* sports editor Ernest Edwards (known as 'Bee') after a hill in South Africa where a Merseyside regiment

Sam Raybould

suffered heavy losses during the Boer War.
The club adopted the city of Liverpool´s Liver bird as the club badge in 1901.
A year earlier the Reds overcame a 5-2 deficit to beat Newcastle United 6-5.

Keeper kit

CARD-STYLE KEEPER

This 1900s image of Sam Hardy is taken from a cigarette-card style image, the woolly jumper and gloves common for the period. Indeed it was during this time that the Football League introduced rules to allow goalkeepers to wear different shirts than the outfield players.

1909-1919

Cup first at the Palace

1909-1919

09/19 PLAYERS Tom Miller, Fred Pagnam
MANAGERS Tom Watson, David Ashworth

ABOUT THE KIT

The main change to the home and away strip for the 1913-14 campaign was the use of a laced turtleneck collar. Red shirt, white baggie shorts and red or black socks remained the home colours, with the away strip being a white shirt with red trim on collar and cuffs, white baggie shorts and black socks. Goalkeepers were also now allowed to wear different shirts than the outfield players (a choice of scarlet red, royal blue or white in 1909-10, with green a further option three seasons later).

Home circa 1914

Home 1909-10

ON-FIELD

Following a disappointing 1908-09 season (finishing 16th), there was huge improvement the following season. Inspired by 30-goal Jack Parkinson, Liverpool finished as First Division runners-up, five points behind Aston Villa. Although subsequent league finishes of 13th, 17th, 12th, 16th and 13th followed before the First World War, the 1913-14 season saw a first FA Cup final appearance, the Reds battling past Barnsley, Gillingham, West Ham, QPR and eventual First Division runners-up Aston Villa before taking on Burnley at Crystal Palace, unfortunately going down 1-0.

OFF-FIELD

From 1915-1919 no league matches were played due to the First World War.

Home circa 1910

FAMOUS MATCH
Aston Villa 0-2 Liverpool (FA Cup semi-final).

LIVERTON 1912

This 1912 team photo was taken ahead of a charity game made up of Liverpool and Everton players.

DID YOU KNOW?

The FA Cup final of 1914, which saw the Reds lose 1-0 to Burnley, was the first time a reigning monarch (King George V) attended the event. The final was also the last to be held at Crystal Palace.

Four Liverpool and four Manchester United players were given life bans for match fixing (1914-15). These sentences were subsequently lifted for the players who took part in the War.

In 1910 Liverpool won the first-ever match at Old Trafford, defeating Manchester United 4-3.

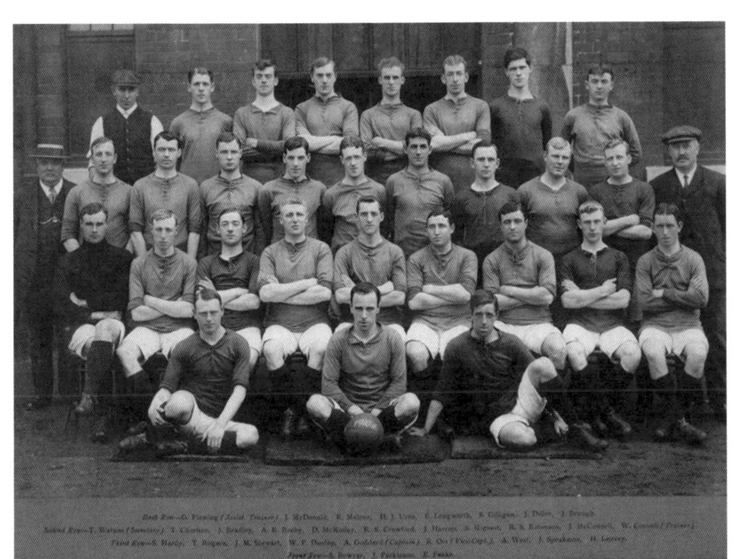

1910 Team

GOALKEEPER KIT

Taken from a cigarette card, Liverpool keeper Ken Campbell sports a green woolly jumper, with black shorts varying from the normal outfield kit.

HOW THEY GOT HERE

BURNLEY | LIVERPOOL

THE CUP HAS BEEN WON BY—

The BEST detailed report of the CUP FINAL will appear in

The Sportsman

BEFORE—

drink to the good fortune of both teams

AND AFTER—

drink to vanquished as well as victors for the gallant fight they both have made—but let your toasts be made in sparkling, delicious

WORTHINGTON'S ALE

W. H. SMITH & SON'S

SOUVENIR CARD

of the

ENGLISH CUP FINAL

1914

BURNLEY v. LIVERPOOL

PLAYED AT THE

CRYSTAL PALACE

1914 FA Cup card

Jack Parkinson

1919-1931

Championship double

1919-1931

19/31 PLAYERS Elisha Scott, Gordon Hodgson
MANAGERS David Ashworth, Matt McQueen, George Patterson

ABOUT THE KIT

There was little change to the home strip during this period, the only difference being the addition of white lining inside the laced collar of the red home shirt.
There was a change to the kit rules though. In the 1921-22 season the away team now had to wear their away strip in the event of a colour clash.

Home 1920s

Home 1926

Home Early 20s

ON-FIELD

With the resumption of League football after the First World War, the club's attendances almost doubled in that first season, 1919-20 in comparision to the last pre-War campaign in 1914-15. The Reds also improved to fourth in Division One and after an identical finish the year after, 1921-22 saw the Championship return to Anfield after a 16-year absence. Defence proved the key for the Reds, who conceded only 36 goals and enjoyed a 30-match spell where they only lost one game, taking the title ahead of Tottenham Hotspur by six points.

A year later and a second successive title was delivered, despite the resignation of David Ashworth mid-term. Having reached the First Division summit in January 1922, Liverpool remained at the top for 16 months, again boosted by a defence who let in 31 goals in 42 games. The winning margin was again six points, Sunderland the runners-up.

In between these title triumphs there was also a FA Charity Shield match against FA Cup holders Huddersfield Town, although the Yorkshire club ran out 1-0 winners. Unfortunately there was to be no more success during the period, with fourth in 1924-25 the club's highest League placing while the FA Cup yielded little success, reaching round five in 1926-27 proving the best Cup run.

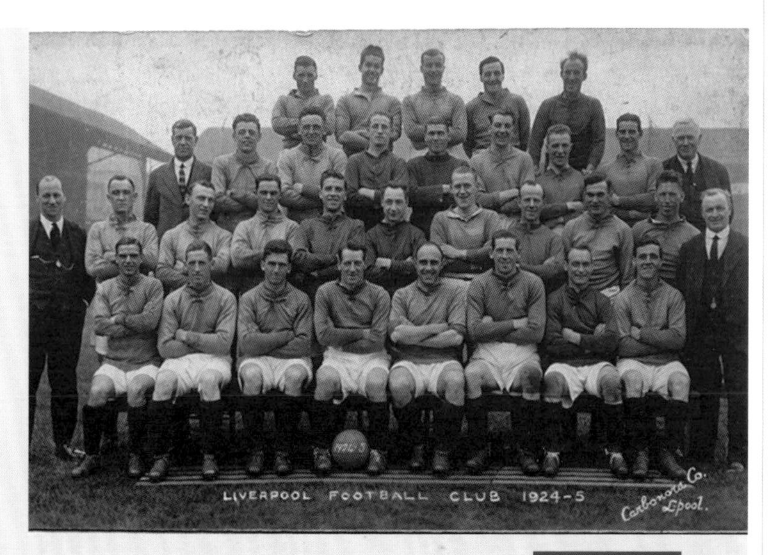

1924-25

OFF-FIELD

David Ashworth became the first Liverpool manager to resign in January, 1923. His replacement was director and former player Matt McQueen, the first time a player had managed and been a director of the club. The 1928-29 season also saw shirt numbers first worn by Arsenal and Chelsea - although this was optional.

FAMOUS MATCH

Liverpool 2-1 Burnley (Division One).

AWAY KIT

Taken from a team picture from 1921-22, the white and red strip also shows some variation in collars - or did some players choose to leave theirs open?

DID YOU KNOW?

The 1922 FA Charity Shield match against Huddersfield Town at Old Trafford was the last to be played at the end of the season - and the first to be played outside London (it was also the first to be played between two teams from the north). Reportedly an original match programme from this match was sold for £2600.

The 1922-23 season saw the Reds win back-to-back First Division titles for the first time.

A new Spion Kop was built with a roof added in the close season of 1928, taking the stand capacity to 30,000.

Season 1930-31 saw Gordon Hodgson set a new club record, scoring 36 goals in 40 games.

GOALKEEPER KIT

The two images of Elisha Scott show the usual thick jumpers of the day, but also suggest a variation in colour – perhaps a black jumper (below) and green (below middle)? Note too on the latter image the trademark kneepads.

Early 20s

Home 1920s

The man in...green?

1931-1935

Black baggies, Hodgson goals and overseas travel

1931-1935

31/35 PLAYERS Gordon Gunson, Berry Nieuwenhuys
MANAGER George Patterson

DID YOU KNOW?

The 1933 FA Cup final between Everton and Manchester City was the first where both teams wore shirt numbers. The Toffees wore 1-11, while City sported 12-22.
Five of the club's biggest-ever league defeats occurred during this period, with the 8-0 reverse at Huddersfield Town in November 1934 being the pick of the results.

ABOUT THE KIT

Although there was little change in either home or away strip during the period, the picture below shows some differences. Taken before the 1935 FA Cup tie at Yeovil Town, the Liverpool skipper (right) sports striped socks while the shirt, including a round collar, also suggests different coloured sleeves.
The other change was to the away kit in 1931-32 with the white away 'baggies' being replaced by black ones.

NUMBERS ON BACK

Below is a scene from the 1933 FA Cup final, a first in English football with player numbers officially worn for the first time.

FAMOUS MATCH

Liverpool 7-4 Everton (Division One).

1932-33

ON-FIELD

The period failed to yield any silverware, although there were goals aplenty in the Liverpool side - and unfortunately against too.
The 1931-32 campaign saw the Reds score 81 goals - the club's fourth highest-ever First Division total, although with 93 conceded they finished 10th.
The next two league seasons saw decline (14th and 18th) before the Reds finished a creditable 7th in 1934-35.
There was little cheer in the FA Cup, with the best season being 1931-32 when Everton, Chesterfield and (First Division) Grimsby Town were seen off before Chelsea claimed a 2-0 win at Anfield.

Away Kit

Home 1935

OFF-FIELD

Despite conceding 88 goals, more than in the previous two seasons when they finished 14th and 18th in the table, Liverpool still managed 7th in the table.

GOALKEEPER KIT

Pictured in 1932 (right), the legendary Elisha Scott was noted for wearing protective knee padding as his distinctive 'uniform.' The traditional jumper came complete with thick collar.

1935-1946

The War years

1935-1946

35/46 PLAYERS Jack Balmer, Willie Fagan, Matt Busby
MANAGERS George Patterson, George Kay

ABOUT THE KIT

A burgundy home kit was introduced in time for the pre-season of 1935-36. The shirt included a collar incorporating two buttons. A season later the away kit design would be changed to match the home strip. The top remained white with red trim, with black baggies and red socks.
Red and white-striped socks became permanent fixtures for both the home and away strips by the 1937-38 season. The post-season tour of 1946 to America also saw Liverpool appear in crew-necked shirts for the first time.

Home 1935-37

Home 1946

ON-FIELD

With the Second World War taking No 1 priority, the period saw only four full seasons completed before the onset of hostilities. They were campaigns when the club failed to shine on the field, Liverpool finishing 19th, 18th, 11th and 11th in the First Divison. That first season saw the club finish only three points above the drop zone, after a run of only three wins in their last 20 games, leading to the departure of manager George Patterson.

The following season League football was suspended indefinitely after only three games.

The FA Cup saw runs to round five in both 1938 and 1939 (going out to Wolves and Huddersfield Town respectively), while 1945-46 saw defeat in round four - 5-2 on aggregate against Bolton Wanderers in the only official games played that season following the War - with league football resuming the following campaign.

Liverpool, 1936-37. Back row (left to right): Mr W.H. Cartwright (director), Berry Nieuwenhuys, Ben Dabbs, Mr G. Richards (director), Alf Hobson, Matt Busby, Fred Rogers, Mr W.J. Harrop (chairman). Front row: Tom Bush, Harry Eastham, Tommy Cooper, Jack Balmer, Alf Hanson.

Home 1936-37

OFF-FIELD

George Patterson stood down as manager in 1936 after a poor end to the season in addition to ill health, although he retained his other position - club secretary.

John McKenna passed away in March 1937, aged 81.

The onset of World War 2 meant that only three games were played at the start of the 1939-40 campaign before the season was abandoned (shirt numbers had actually been introduced for this season). Resultedly, between September 3rd, 1939 and August 30th, 1946 there were no league matches played.

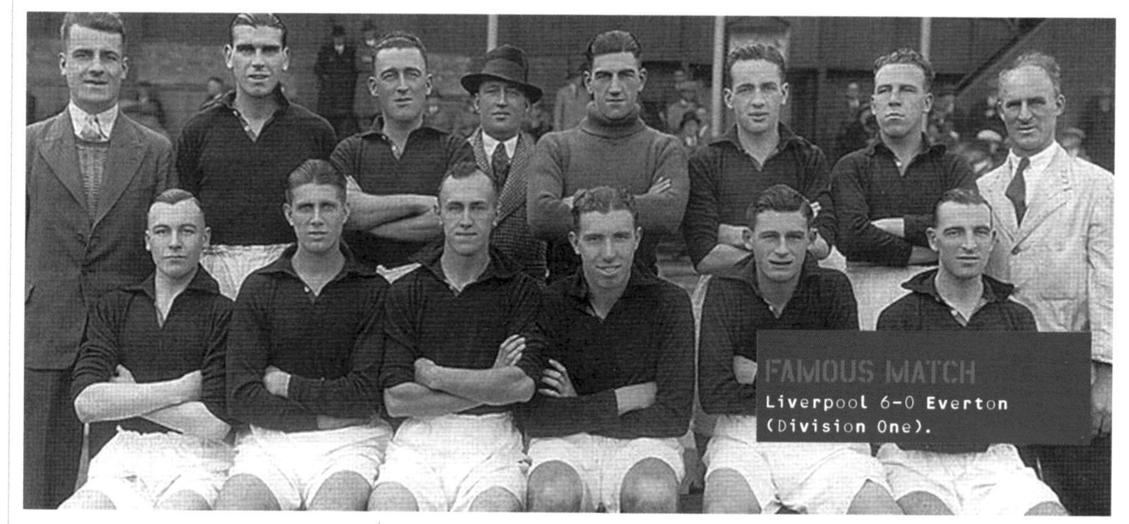

FAMOUS MATCH

Liverpool 6–0 Everton (Division One).

US TOUR '46

Billy Liddell sporting a change strip on the club's post-season tour to America.

REDS NO 9

Action shot of the new numbered shirts, again from the same tour.

DID YOU KNOW?

The new post-War strip was the first shirt with short sleeves.
George Kay was the first full-time Liverpool manager.
Gordon Hodgson's 10-year Reds career ended in 1936, and he retains the record of having scored the most hat-tricks for the club – 17.
A certain William Shankly appeared once for Liverpool during the Second World War as a guest player.

US Tour '46

Strangely the Reds played Chelsea on the opening day of three of these four seasons. Following a 2-2 away draw in 1935-36, the first game of both 1937-38 and 1938-39 saw wildly contrasting fortunes. At Stamford Bridge in 37-38 it was a day to forget as the home side eased to a 6-1 triumph. But the following season at Anfield, revenge was gained courtesy of a 2-1 win.

The 1945-46 FA Cup was the first and only season when the competition became a two legged affair up to the quarter-final. This was brought in due to official League football not resuming until the following season.

GOALKEEPER KIT

The knee pads are in place although the unfamiliar white was a first. The short sleeves could be attributed to the occasion - a friendly being played on the Canary Islands in 1935.

1946-1953

Wembley first and a Liver bird on our shirt

1946-1953

46/53 PLAYERS Albert Stubbins, Bob Paisley
MANAGERS George Kay, Don Welsh

Original number stitched on Billy Liddell's shirt (circa 1950, right), as displayed in the Liverpool club museum.

Original early 50s

ABOUT THE KIT

Shirt numbers were now made compulsory, and with the onset of the first league season after the War, Liverpool made alterations to both home and away strips. Both shirts now had white lining on the button section on the collar. The 'baggies' remained white for home and black for away, while the home and away strips utilised red and white-striped socks.

Home 51-52

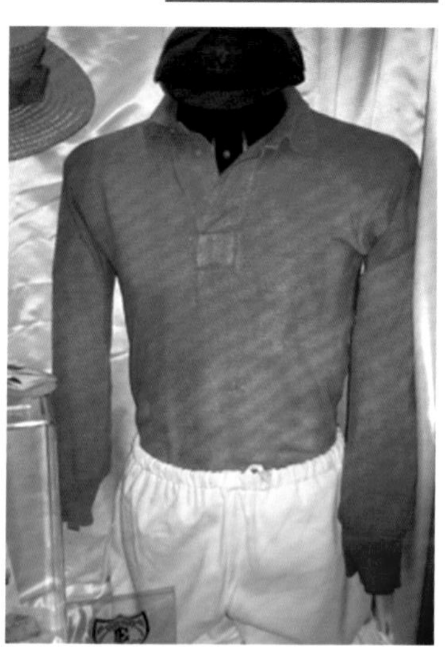

Original early 50s

ON-FIELD

The Football League returned to full competitive action in 1946-47, the FA Cup having began again the season before). Subsequently it would be a memorable one for the club, and the peak of these seven seasons. Despite an inferior goal difference to the other sides who finished in the top four, the Reds claimed the First Division just a point ahead of Wolves and Manchester United. Indeed, Liverpool won 2-1 at Molineux in their final league game in May, although because of a severe winter, Stoke City in fourth could still take the title on goal difference by winning their last match against Sheffield United – the game taking place on June 14th! But the Potters blew it, going down 2-1 and Liverpool had claimed the first post-War title.

The club also enjoyed a run to the FA Cup semi-finals that season, eventually losing 1-0 to Burnley in a replay at Maine Road, Manchester. Surprisingly, given the emergence of Albert Stubbins and Billy Liddell, the Reds spent the rest of the 1946-53 period languishing in mid-table – with 8th in 1949-50 their highest finish after such a good start to the campaign. However, this season saw an appearance at Wembley, as the Reds battled through to the FA Cup final to face Arsenal. Unfortunately, a first triumph eluded the club, the Gunners winning 2-0.

Close season 1951

OFF-FIELD

Jack Pickering wrote his name in Liverpool folklore as a result of his match-winner for Sheffield United against Stoke in June 1947. The 40-year-old, in only his first league appearance of the season, scored the goal that ended the Potters' title dreams – and confirmed a fifth league crown for the Reds.

FAMOUS MATCH

Liverpool 2-0 Everton (FA Cup semi-final).

FIRST NUMBER

With shirt numbers now compulsory, this No 7 from 1946-47 seems tiny compared with future designs.

1950 FA CUP FINAL

Albert Stubbins' 1950 FA Cup final shirt as displayed in the club museum - complete with dried blood stains!

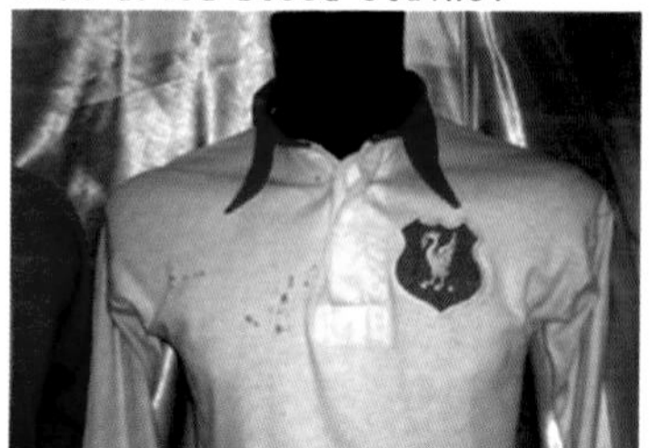

DID YOU KNOW?

The Reds went the first 19 games of the 1949-50 season unbeaten - but still finished only 8th.

Arsenal captain (and former Everton favourite) Joe Mercer still lived on Merseyside and trained at Liverpool regularly. But when the Reds were paired with the Gunners for the 1950 FA Cup final, Mercer had to change his arrangements...he was forced to train at the far

1950 FA Cup final

end of the pitch, on his own.
In good condition, the 1950 FA Cup final programme is worth £150, while original tickets can sell for £50+.
Bill Shankly was shortlisted for the manager's job before Welsh got the job.
Jack Balmer scored three hat-tricks in three successive games during the 1946-47 season – a League record.

Away 50-51

GOALKEEPER KIT

Two variations on the goalkeeping `uniform' of the day. The top picture is from 1950-51 while the other (bottom), is Cyril Sidlow's 1950 FA Cup jumper, complete with Liver bird badge – a Liverpool first for keepers?

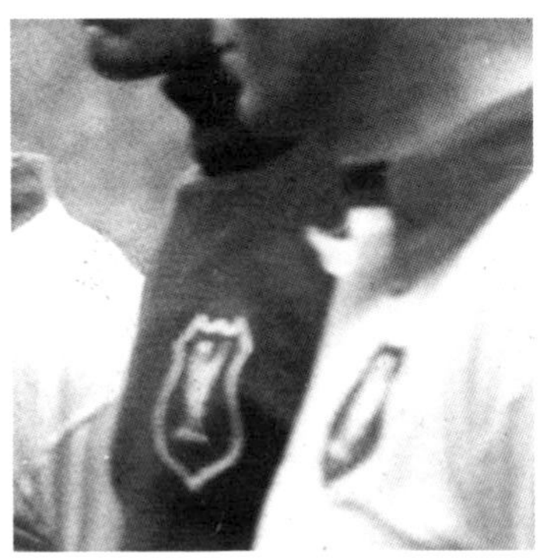

1953-1955

Relegation woes at Anfield

1953-1955

53/55 PLAYERS Alan A'Court, Sammy Smyth
MANAGER Don Welsh

ABOUT THE KIT

A new home kit welcomed Liverpudlians in time for the 1953-54 season. The home version incorporated a white stand collar and two button front. The 'baggies' could now be described as shorts (which remained white), while the socks were red with white stripes. The away kit was the same as that used in previous seasons, incorporating the LFC crest design and a red stand collar. Shorts were black while the home socks were used as part of the strip.

Away 53-54

Home 53-54

ON-FIELD

Taking into account the significance of what happened, the 1953-54 campaign must rate as the worst in the club's history. Liverpool finished rock bottom in the First Division, the team failing to recover from a run of only five wins in their first 24 games. The mixture of veterans and grafters (with the superhuman efforts of Billy Liddell aside) proved ill-equipped to survive. To make matters worse, the relegated Reds effectively swapped places with neighbours Everton, who were promoted at the same time.
The following season in Division Two, a hoped-for promotion challenge failed to materialise, with Liverpool eventually limping home in 11th with a 6-1 final-day defeat at Rotherham United indicating that things needed to improve.
The run to the fifth round of the FA Cup in 1955 did at least provide some joy for the red half of Merseyside, as First Division Everton were swept aside 4-0 at Goodison Park in round four.

OFF-FIELD

John Evans is one of only four Liverpool players to score five goals in a game, the forward achieving the feat against Bristol Rovers in September 1954.

53-54

FAMOUS MATCH

Everton 0-4 Liverpool (FA Cup).

NUMBERS ON BACK

The No 9 shirt of Liverpool from season 1953-54.

LFC CREST

Worn on the shirt in the 1950 FA Cup final, the badge was a regular feature of the away jerseys during the period.

DID YOU KNOW?

In three games between December 12 and December 25, the Reds conceded 15 goals – five in each match – losing 5-1, 5-1 and 5-2.

April 19th, 1954 was Billy Liddell's last goal in the First Division, the Reds legend scoring the fourth in a 4-1 victory over Middlesbrough at Anfield. The Teessiders were, like Liverpool, also already relegated at that stage.

54-55

GOALKEEPER KIT

Despite being August at Bolton in 1953, Reds keeper Charlie Ashcroft doesn't seem too concerned. The defender is Ray Lambert (note variation in socks) while the original caption made reference to Ashcroft 'standing guard' and Lambert 'letting it go out of play.' That said, Liverpool still went down 2-0.

The 1954 World Cup was the first in which players were given shirt numbers. Liverpool lost to Birmingham City 9-1 on 11th December, 1954. It is noted as the club's biggest-ever defeat.

53-54

1955-1959

Collars, V-necks and Division Two

1955-1959

55/59 PLAYERS Billy Liddell, Geoff Twentyman
MANAGERS Don Welsh, Phil Taylor

ABOUT THE KIT

The home shirt changed to a single buttoned white stand collar, with red cuffs in time for the 1955-56 season, a kit which would be used for at least three seasons.
It was also around this period, possibly the following season, that the first Liverpool V-neck strip was introduced. The red shirt, less baggy than its previous incarnation, incorporated white cuffs and collar, with short sleeves becoming the norm. The shorts remained white with red trim, with the socks remaining unchanged from the previous post-War years.
A new away kit was also brought in, which was again a white shirt, black shorts (although when shorts clashed, the home white shorts were used) and white socks. A red trim was prominent on the shirt collar and cuffs.
Research has uncovered match images that suggest the baggy kit was used again despite the introduction of the classic V-neck Liverpool strip. These pictures (right) show the Reds in action in two different kits during the 1957-58 FA Cup run. Above right shows third-round action from Southend United v Liverpool, while the other image is from the quarter-final at Blackburn Rovers.

V-neck, '58

Baggy, '58

ON-FIELD

Finishes of 3rd, 3rd, 4th and 4th showed that the club was regularly in the hunt for promotion back to the First Division, but that they were not yet good enough to make the leap. In 1956-57, with Don Welsh having been replaced by Phil Taylor towards the end of 1955-56, they finished just a point behind second-placed Nottingham Forest, who went up instead (the team having recorded their best goal difference in a decade). Despite coming 4th the season after, the top four were seperated by only three points. This season (1957-58) also saw the Reds reach the FA Cup quarter-finals, eventually going down 2-1 to Blackburn Rovers.

Firsts v Reserves, 56-57

OFF-FIELD

Don Welsh became the first-ever Liverpool manager to be sacked in 1956, Welsh having presided over the club's fall from Division One and subsequent failure to achieve promotion in their first two seasons in Division Two.

Away action, 57-58

FAMOUS MATCH

Worcester C. 2-1 Liverpool (FA Cup).

LIVERPOOL REPLICA

Although this 1950s replica was used at the turn of the decade, the oval-style badge was only ever used on the white-collar kit.

BADGE...NO BADGE

Other research has shown up matches where a Liverpool away shirt without badge was worn - the example on the right is from a game at Barnsley in March 1956.

DID YOU KNOW?

Liverpool's FA Cup third-round defeat at non-league Worcester City in January 1959 is deemed as one of the worst in the club's history. It would prove a turning point for the Reds though, with Taylor being dismissed the following season, to be replaced by a certain Bill Shankly.

GOALKEEPER KIT

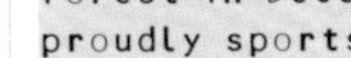

Tommy Younger, shown here in flying form at Nottingham Forest in December 1956, proudly sports the Liver bird crest on his jumper.

58-59

55-56

56-57

1959-1962

Shankly, a Colossus and promotion

1959-1962

59/62 PLAYERS Roger Hunt, Gordon Milne, Kevin Lewis
MANAGERS Phil Taylor, Bill Shankly

Home 59-60

Away 59-60

ABOUT THE KIT

The 1959-60 season saw a small change to the home kit, with the striped socks changed to white with red tops. The home shorts were again also worn with the away kit, as an alternative to the black shorts - an occurrence that would become more common in future seasons.

ON-FIELD

The club entered their sixth season in the Second Division under the tutorlage of former player Phil Taylor, although with another faltering promotion bid overshadowing the club's ambitions, a new man was brought in. Huddersfield Town had been making waves thanks to the efforts of a talented group of players, and their manager Bill Shankly was asked to take over at Anfield.
His first official game in charge did little to impress the masses and inspire confidence - Cardiff City coming away from Anfield with a 4-0 success - although improvements followed, and Liverpool finished 3rd, although well off the pace of the two promotion places.
The following season, 1960-61 and it was again a case of gradual improvement. The Reds' points tally grew and they finished closer to the top two in terms of points - but again, third was not good enough. Shankly knew what was required - and the signings of Ron Yeats and Ian St John proved inspired. Unbeaten at home, Liverpool romped to the Division Two title, finishing eight points ahead of runners-up Leyton Orient, while the Reds also enjoyed a run to the fifth round of the FA Cup, beating Chelsea and Oldham before going down to Preston North End in a second replay. But the Cup could wait - the Reds were back in the big time.

Team 61-62

OFF-FIELD

Billy Liddell retired in 1961 after playing 537 games for the club, scoring 229 goals. Peter Thompson's speculative 30-yarder for Preston had knocked the Reds out of the FA Cup in 1962 - by August 1963 he would be a Liverpool player.

FAMOUS MATCH

Liverpool 0-4 Cardiff City (Division Two).

NUMBERS ON BACK

The style sported by the Reds during the 1961-62 season.

EMBROIDERED BADGE

As sported on the red home shirt, this from 1959.

DID YOU KNOW?

Dave Hickson was Phil Taylor's last signing in November 1959.
Bill Shankly was the first Liverpool manager to have full control over on-field affairs - the team having previously been picked - as was common - by the board of directors.
Having taken part in the League Cup in 1960-61, the Reds did not enter the tournament again until 1967.

Home 61-62

GOALKEEPER KIT

Two images taken from the 1960-61 campaign reflect the simple nature of the keeper's lot – a basic jumper and no gloves!

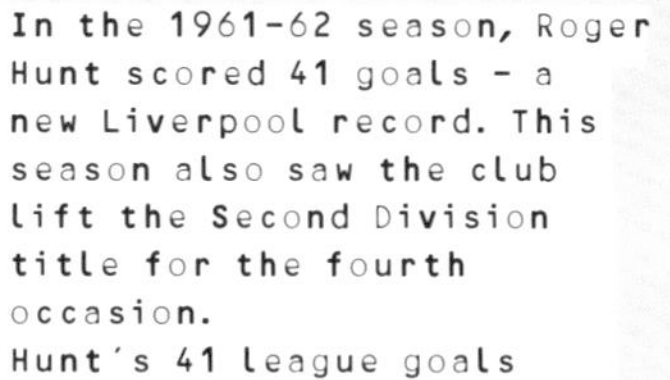

In the 1961-62 season, Roger Hunt scored 41 goals – a new Liverpool record. This season also saw the club lift the Second Division title for the fourth occasion.
Hunt's 41 league goals remain a club record – the season would see Liverpool score 99.

Away 60-61

1962-1964

Back in the big time – and champions at last

1962-1964

62/64 PLAYERS Ron Yeats, Peter Thompson
MANAGER Bill Shankly

ABOUT THE KIT

The Reds' first season back in the top flight since 1953-54 also signalled a change in shirt design, from V-neck to crew neck. However, as the lead-in photo shows, some of the squad in the team photo line-up were left to make do with the previous season's baggier kit.

Home kit 62-64

ON-FIELD

On the back of promotion, Liverpool made a big impact in their first season back in the top flight. Expectations weren't too high, but with Shankly at the helm, the Reds were able to dismiss such fears. Failing to win their last three league games cost Liverpool a place or two, ending up 8th in the table although they also reached the FA Cup semi-final, where hopes of a first FA Cup final success were ended by Leicester City, 1-0 at Hillsborough.

The following season, 1963-64, saw the club really signal their place back amongst the big boys. Despite losing the first three home games of the season, a run of seven consecutive victories in March and April, which culminated in a 5-0 demolition of Arsenal, saw the Reds to their 6th Championship - and the club's first for 17 years. In the process the club were to be admitted to Europe, in the form of the European Cup, for the very first time. A new era had begun.

Champions '64

OFF-FIELD

Following the club's third Anfield defeat from three games of the 1963-64 campaign, Shankly told the Liverpool board: "I assure you, gentlemen, that before the end of the season we will win a home game!"

Home 62-63

FAMOUS MATCH

Liverpool 5-0 Arsenal (Division One).

YOUNG CALLY

Ian Callaghan had now become a Liverpool regular, having made his debut as an 18-year-old in 1960.

PENALTY KING

Jim Furnell, here in action for the Reds, actually saved two penalties against his former club for Arsenal during 1963-64.

DID YOU KNOW?

Jim Furnell penalty saves came in the FA Cup, and in Division One. The first save, in the Reds' 1-0 FA Cup fifth-round win at Highbury came from Roger Hunt - who never took another penalty for the club. The other was from Ian Callaghan in April that season. Fortunately the Reds were already 5-0 up, and clinched the title that day!

Away kit, 1964

GOALKEEPER, NO...?

Bert Slater was less than 5ft 9ins tall, but played his part to help the Reds reach the top flight. Here he is in action at Brighton, with his goalkeeper 'jumper' shy of a number.

1964-1967

Cup first, champions...and Europe

1964-1967

64/67 PLAYERS Ian St John, Gerry Byrne, Chris Lawler
MANAGER Bill Shankly

ABOUT THE KIT

The biggest single alteration to Liverpool's home strip during the 20th century occurred during the 1964-65 campaign, and all because of the influence of manager Bill Shankly. The story goes that Shankly asked his then skipper Ron Yeats to try on an all-red strip at Anfield. After fulfilling the request, Yeats went in search of Shankly and he emerged from the tunnel to see the Reds boss in the middle of the pitch, who uttered the immortal line: "Christ son, you look about seven foot tall, we're going to play in all-red from now on."
That said, later in the season white shorts and socks were still worn in some games as shown (far right) from this action shot in February 1965, although by the time of the 1965 FA Cup final, all red was the norm.

Our research also uncovered evidence that the club may also have sported yellow during this period. Although only in black and white, the shot above was taken from the European Cup home clash against Ajax in December 1966. With European rules deeming that the home team should use a change strip should a clash of colours occur, the Amsterdam side wore their usual red and white while Liverpool, unable to use the red home or white second kit were presumably forced into said re-think - yellow shirt and socks with black shorts.

Home 65-66

ON-FIELD

A second First Division title in three seasons was claimed in 1965-66, a success that rounded off a glittering spell which also included the club's first-ever FA Cup final victory in 1965, fulfilling a Shankly mission upon his appointment - to add the trophy to the club's previously barren Cup trophy haul. The 2-1 extra-time defeat of Leeds United was made all the more remarkable as Gerry Byrne played on having broken his collarbone in the first half of the match, even setting up the winning goal for Ian St John. It was an exciting period for the Reds, who also made their European debut in 1964-65, a European Cup campaign that would end in cruel 4-3 aggregate defeat at the hands of Inter Milan in the semi-finals, this after the Reds had won the Anfield first leg 3-1.

A year later and Liverpool went a step further, reaching the final this time in the European Cup Winners' Cup where Borussia Dortmund were the opponents at Hampden Park. Unfortunately, the favourites failed at the final hurdle, going down 2-1 after extra time.

Other silverware did arrive at Anfield during these three seasons, namely the FA Charity Shield in 1966 (a 1-0 victory over Everton at Goodison Park), while it was shared in `64 and `65.

Away kits 66-67

OFF-FIELD

Phil Chisnall, in making his Liverpool debut in the FA Charity Shield in August 1964, became the first substitute used in a competitive game for the club. At that stage it was deemed that a change could only be made to an injured player, the man in question being Alf Arrowsmith.

FAMOUS MATCH

Liverpool 2-1 Leeds United (FA Cup final).

PHOTOCALL

Tommy Smith (below, left) and Roger Hunt wait in line, 1966.

WEMBLEY '65

Two versions of the original commemorative badge.

DID YOU KNOW?

The all-red strip was first used in a European Cup tie against Anderlecht, which the Reds won 3-0. 1964-65 was also the club's first season of European competition. That season also produced another first when the Reds' home clash with Arsenal became the first to be screened by the BBC's *Match Of The Day* on August 22, 1964.

66-67

John Sealey's Liverpool first-team career began and ended on April 26, 1965. With players rested ahead of the FA Cup final five days later, Sealey scored the second goal in a 3-1 win at Wolves. He did not play again, leaving him with a 100% goal record for the club.
Only 14 players were used in the first team in the 1965-66 season.

66-67 No 10

GOALKEEPER KIT

Liverpool's first genuine successor to the legendary Elisha Scott, Tommy Lawrence was a regular presence between the posts in the 1960s. Here he sports a top more reminiscent to a jumper, complete with oval badge.

1967-1972

So near, yet so far

1967-1972

67/72 PLAYERS Tommy Smith, Alun Evans, Steve Heighway
MANAGER Bill Shankly

Home shirt, 1967-68

Home shirt, 1971-72

ABOUT THE KIT

Although the kit remained largely unchanged, the oval shape around the Liver bird badge was eventually removed, with an embroidered Liver bird (in white) replacing it on the home shirt (and in red on the white away shirt). Red, and white socks were used for home and away strips respectively, with black, white or red shorts optional away from home.
One doubt encountered in our research is shown on page 83 - namely the shirt and socks used at Arsenal in 1967-68. Is it the usual white or slightly darker, maybe yellow? This similar descrepency cropped up against Ajax in 1966 (see page 74).

Home replica, 1968-69

ON-FIELD

A period of near misses proved the theme as Shankly's run of silverware as Reds boss ended - for the time being. Liverpool were First Division runners-up in 1968-69, FA Cup runners-up and Inter-cities Fairs Cup semi-finalists in 1971 and also FA Charity Shield runners-up later that year. There was certainly no struggle in the league during this time, as the Reds enjoyed top-five finishes in each of the seasons although the semi-final aside, there was general failure in European competition and the League Cup.

There was also one noticeable result in the FA Cup the year before the run to Wembley in '71. A shock quarter-final defeat at Third Division Watford is said to have signalled the break-up of Shankly's first great Liverpool side, a decision that was to reap dividends in future seasons.

Away 1967-68

OFF-FIELD

1967-68 saw Liverpool return to the League Cup for the first time since 1960-61. However, it was an inauspicious return, the Reds going down to Bolton Wanderers in a second-round replay.

Away 1968-69

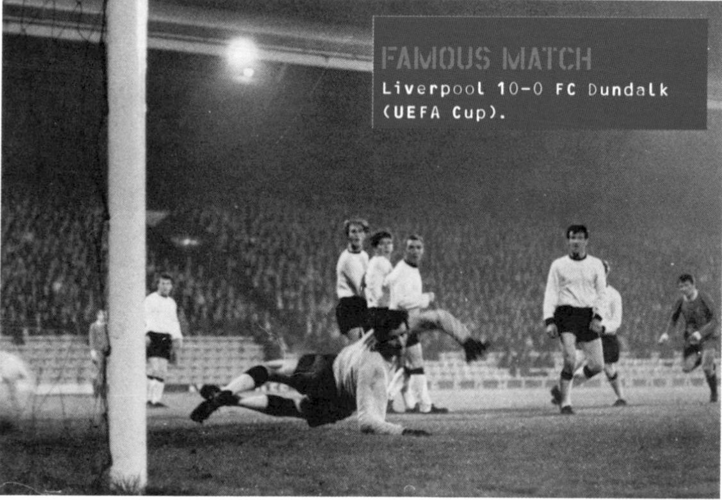

FAMOUS MATCH

Liverpool 10-0 FC Dundalk (UEFA Cup).

CHANGING OF THE GUARD

Out went Tommy Lawrence's plain goalkeeper's jersey, and in came the Ray Clemence 'Liver bird' of the 1970s.

THOSE TRAINING TOPS

Made famous during the 1960s, the 'Liverpool FC' tops were regularly sported at Melwood.

DID YOU KNOW?

Alun Evans became the first £100,000 teenager when he signed for the club in 68-69. The Reds went out of the Inter-cities Fairs Cup at the first-round stage to Athletic Bilbao on the toss of a coin, the last time this method was used to decide a European tie. The away goals rule would be used instead. Roger Hunt, who retired in 1969, still holds the club's league goalscoring record.

At Arsenal 67-68 - White top?

Away 68-69

MODEL APPROACH

A more pleasing scene than normal, as the famous red shirt is modelled circa. 1971-72 season.

1972-1973

Double delight for Shankly

1972-1973

KIT DESIGN Umbro

72/73 PLAYERS Kevin Keegan, Ian Callaghan

MANAGER Bill Shankly

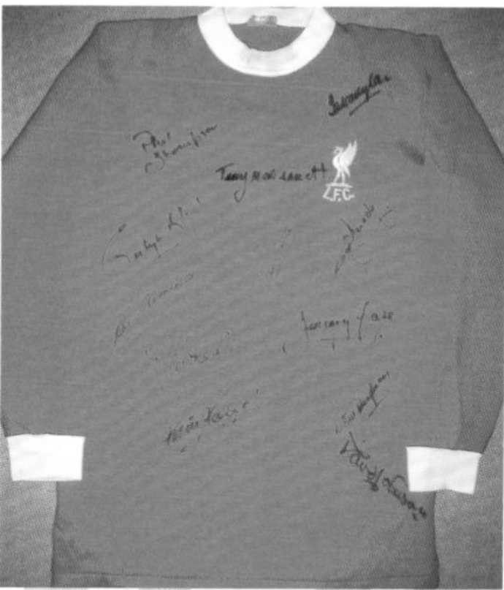

ABOUT THE KIT

For the first time Liverpool's strip was produced by an official sports manufacturer in the form of Umbro. However, there is no evidence to suggest that the kit was ever worn with the kit designer's logo shown, with pictures gathered from the *Liverpool Daily Post & Echo* archive showing no logos on either shirt or shorts from this season. That said, original kits of the period are complete with Umbro labels.

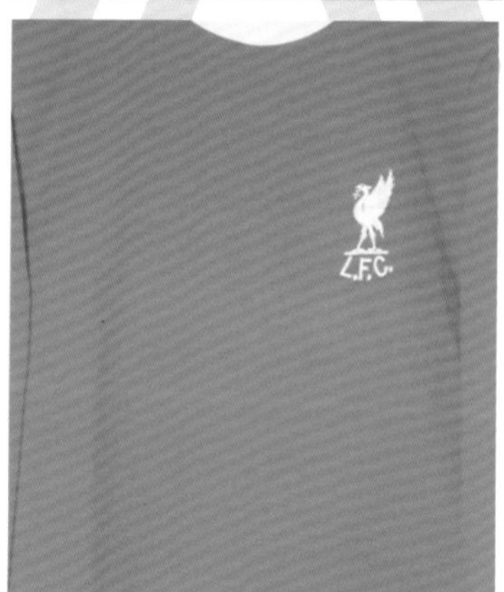

Home kit

ON-FIELD

Liverpool ended their barren Championship spell in 1973, claiming a first title in seven years to hold off the challenge of Arsenal by three points. It was the realisation that Shankly had built a second great team, and also ended Emlyn Hughes' jinx – 'Crazyhorse' having not won the First Division during his spell at Anfield until then.
Despite disappointment in the FA Cup and League Cup (exits at rounds four and five respectively), there was to be double success come the season's end.
The Reds' run to the UEFA Cup final included a semi-final victory over Tottenham Hotspur, sweet revenge after the Londoners had knocked the Reds out of the League Cup.
The final pitted the club against West Germans Borussia Moenchengladbach. The first leg at Anfield went according to plan, a 3-0 win all but securing the trophy. Kevin Keegan scored two of the goals, and he could have had a third on the night, but for missing a spot-kick (Ray Clemence also saved a penalty that night from the Germans' Jupp Heynckes).
However, far from easing through in the second leg, the Germans hit back with two first-half goals from Heynckes. But the Reds somehow managed to hold off their hosts and claim the trophy 3-2 on aggregate.

Action 72-73

OFF-FIELD

The Main Stand/Paddock was redeveloped to incorporate a new roof.
Ray Clemence's penalty save in the UEFA Cup final, first leg was all down to a bit of homework: "I watched Heynckes take a penalty in the semi-final on television and decided to dive the same way."

1972-1973

UMBRO '73

Despite the absence of a shirt logo, the great Bill Shankly sported the Umbro diamond on his Liverpool tracksuit top following the UEFA success.

FAMOUS MATCH

Liverpool 3-0 Borussia M'gladbach (UEFA Cup final).

UEFA CUP '73

A ticket from the second leg in Germany (a green one - there are two different types) sold for over £800 while the programme has fetched £300 in the past.

KEEPER JERSEY

The simple dark green and white crest of 1972-73.

DID YOU KNOW?

Future England forward Frank Worthington had all but sealed a move to the club in 1972 before a medical revealed 'high blood pressure' - and the move was called off, with Leicester City stepping in. Ironically the day the title was sealed Worthington was in the Foxes side at Anfield.

The UEFA Cup final, first leg programme is worth around £25, a ticket up to £50.

HUNT TESTIMONIAL

No less a figure than West Ham and England World Cup-winning captain Bobby Moore was spotted in the unfamiliar white of Liverpool – although it was all for a good cause. It was April 1972 and over 55,000 turned out for Roger Hunt's testimonial, with Liverpool's 1965 FA Cup-winning side defeating Moore's England XI 8-6.

Mix-and-match

SHADES OF WHITE

When colour clashes occurred with Liverpool's usual away strip of white shirt with red collar, black shorts and white socks (left), there were no third kits. There was simply a more 'mix-and-match' policy with the home kit often used. A case in point was the kit below, with white shorts and the red home socks worn.

MIDLAND BANK
BET WITH JOE CORAL

1973-1976

Wembley, Europe...and the end of an era

1973-1976

KIT DESIGN Umbro

73/76 PLAYERS John Toshack, Peter Cormack
MANAGERS Bill Shankly, Bob Paisley

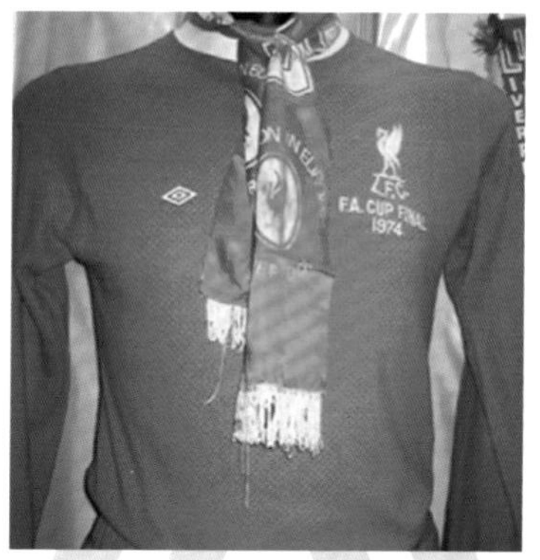

'74 FA Cup final

ABOUT THE KIT

The Umbro logo became a permanent fixture on the strips in 1973-74 - although there is evidence to suggest that the Liver bird remained the only addition to the shirt during games that season. Black shorts and white socks were worn with the away kit, with white shorts again optional, mainly when colours clashed.
The badges, in a perforated material, became an orange/yellow colour on both the home and away kit in the latter years of the period, with a blue/black/white Umbro being used for much of 1974-75.

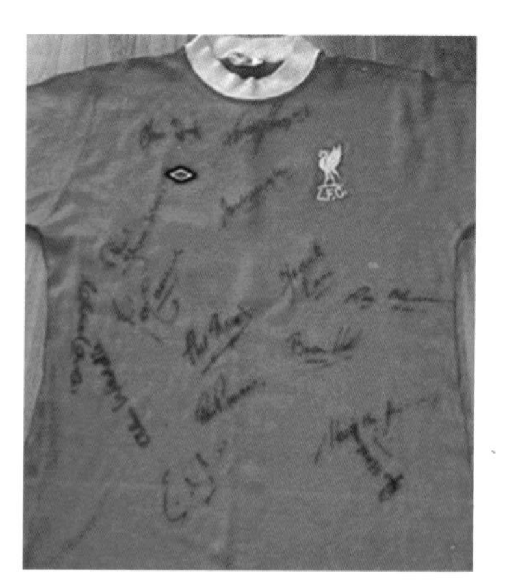

74-75 home

There are also versions of this shirt with the Umbro incorporating 'red', rather than the blue colour.

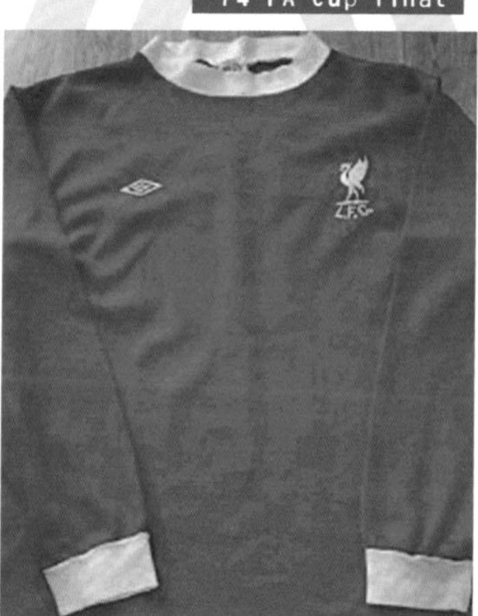

75-76 home

ON-FIELD

Having been runners-up in the First Division in Bill Shankly's last season in charge (1974) and then again in 1975, Bob Paisley finally claimed his first trophy as Reds boss in the form of the title, stamping his mark at Anfield. The silverware was collected at the climax of the season, with a two-legged UEFA Cup final against FC Bruges sandwiched in between. The first game at Anfield proved a nightmare in the first half, with the Belgians leading 2-0. But a change at half-time, with Jimmy Case coming on for John Toshack sparked a revival, with Case himself netting the equaliser in a 3-2 victory.

In between the second leg, there was the small matter of the destiny of the First Division to be decided. With QPR top by a point having played all their games, Liverpool needed to win at relegated Wolves to guarantee the title. The Midlands side led 1-0 with 15 minutes to go, and the dream appeared to be slipping. But Keegan, Toshack and Ray Kennedy struck to break the hearts of QPR.

There was still a second UEFA Cup triumph to chase, with the second leg in Belgium being played three weeks after the Anfield game. The Reds began poorly, with a Bruges penalty giving the home side the advantage after 10 minutes courtesy of the away goals rule, but Kevin Keegan hit back just four minutes later. A spirited fightback ensued for the Belgians, but a determined rearguard effort proved key for the Reds, who claimed the trophy 4-3 on aggregate. It would be an experience that would stand them in good stead for the following season.

Other on-field highlights of the period included a memorable FA Cup triumph over Newcastle United in 1974, and then the subsequent FA Charity Shield meeting with Leeds United that August, memorable for Bill Shankly leading out Liverpool for the last time at Wembley – and Keegan and Billy Bremner being sent off for fighting. The eventual winners? The Reds in a penalty shootout after a 1-1 draw.

OFF-FIELD

Bill Shankly's shock retirement in the summer of 1974 overshadowed the club. Having built his second great Liverpool team, he confirmed that the FA Charity Shield would be his last game in charge – with his assistant Bob Paisley taking over.

'74 FA Charity Shield

1973-1976

Shanks' last game, 1974

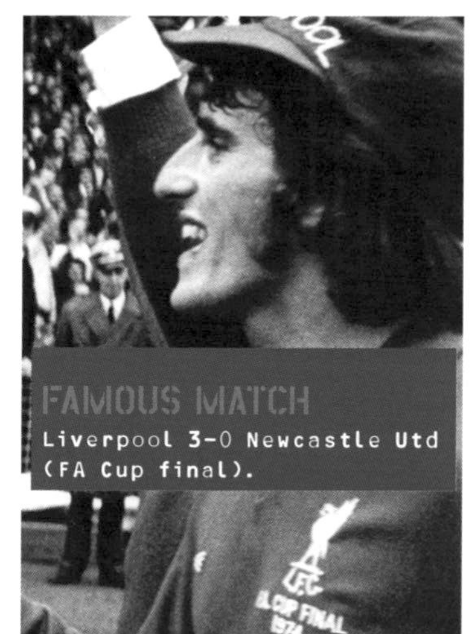

FAMOUS MATCH

Liverpool 3-0 Newcastle Utd (FA Cup final).

UMBRO LOGO

The black/white/blue diamond was an unusual addition worn during part of the 74-75 season, although usually it was the white that was most common during the period.

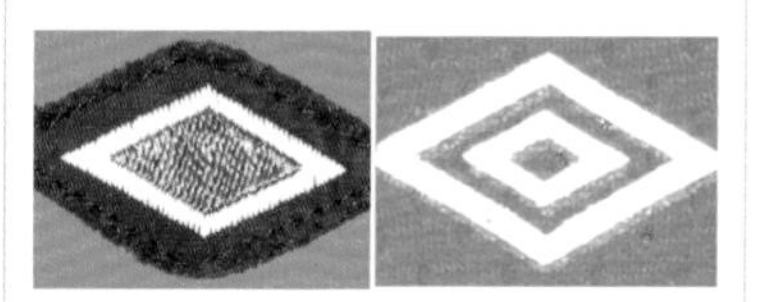

FA CUP FINAL '74

A classic logo which became more prominent in years to come in finals. The programme from the game is worth around £5, the ticket maybe double.

DID YOU KNOW?

Youngsters Alan Kennedy and Terry McDermott were in the Newcastle United team swept aside by the Reds in the 1974 FA Cup final.

Roy Evans joined Ronnie Moran in the Anfield boot room in 1974-75.

The 11-0 win over Stromgodset in the European Cup Winners' Cup first round, first leg in September 1974 is a club record.

All white away

The 1974 FA Charity Shield clash against Leeds was the first played at Wembley (ticket and programme is valued at £5).
It was claimed that Middlesbrough's John Hickton lost five teeth when Liverpool's Joey Jones took him out and got sent off in the Reds' 1-0 win in November that season. For his sins Jones was banned for...one match.

White and black away

KIT TECHNOLOGY

Coming three years after the FA Cup final defeat to Arsenal, Bill Shankly insisted on an improved kit that would give his men the edge in hot conditions - just like the Gunners had enjoyed against his team. The dummy below was exhibited to show off this 'state-of-the-art' shirt, with its perforated design.

UMBRO CHANGES 73-76

PLAIN GREEN

The goalkeeper kit remained without thrills, with many other teams adopting similar styles of a solid green or yellow.

DATSU

1976-1978

Champions of Europe

1976-1978

KIT DESIGN Umbro

76/78 PLAYERS Kenny Dalglish, David Fairclough

MANAGER Bob Paisley

ABOUT THE KIT

The most prominent changes to the kits during this period were to the collar, and to the Umbro logo. The classic V-neck was re-introduced to the red shirt, while the Umbro logo became bigger on the shirts – while on the white away shirt the colours of the badges became red (although it is not certain whether the team still wore the gold/yellow alternatives after this period). The classic style of the home kit would remain unchanged for six years until 1982, with a simple white V-neck and cuffs.

'77 Rome

Home (front and back)

ON-FIELD

Although a close-run title race ended successfully in 1976-77 (the Reds were runners-up a year later), it was Europe that dominated these two seasons. The highlight of the 1976-77 European Cup campaign would be a quarter-final against St Etienne, the runners-up from the previous season. The 1-0 first-leg deficit was quickly wiped out at Anfield by Kevin Keegan, but once the Frenchmen levelled Liverpool needed to score two goals to go through. Ray Kennedy put the Reds 2-1 up before six minutes from time `super sub' David Fairclough earned himself a place in Kop folklore - the dream continued. FC Zurich were swept aside in the semi-finals before Borussia Moenchengladbach and the final in Rome. A memorable occasion, and a memorable result as Liverpool triumphed 3-1 to claim the trophy - this coming just four days after an agonising 2-1 defeat to Manchester United in the FA Cup final at Wembley, treble dreams ending in an instant.

The 1977-78 season would also end in European triumph, this following a campaign which saw a first European Super Cup success (7-1 on aggregate over Kevin Keegan's Hamburg) and a first League Cup final (the Reds going down 1-0 to Nottingham Forest in a replay). Following aggregate wins over Dynamo Dresden, Benfica and Moenchengladbach again, FC Bruges were the finalists at Wembley. Hot favourites Liverpool struggled to break down the defensive Belgians before new hero Kenny Dalglish's famous `dink' over the onrushing keeper secured a second successive triumph.

OFF-FIELD

Record fees were paid out for Kenny Dalglish (£440,000 to Celtic in August 1977, a British record) and Graeme Souness (£352,000 to Middlesbrough, a record fee between two English clubs) within six months.
In June 1977, Kevin Keegan became the most expensive British footballer when he joined Hamburg for £500,000.

Away - the socks vary...

EURO LOGOS

The distinctive, rounded 1977 Rome badge was replaced by a more sober design a year later for the Wembley showpiece.

FAMOUS MATCH

Liverpool 3-1 St Etienne (European Cup quarter-final).

CUP FINAL BADGES

Keeping the same theme as Wembley '78, the final shirts retained the simple Liver bird of the usual LFC shirt.

DID YOU KNOW?

The Reds became the first British team to successfully defend the European Cup.

Phil Neal played in 417 consective games, from 1976 through to 1983.

Having won the FA Charity Shield in 1976, beating Southampton, the 1977 match saw a 0-0 draw against Cup holders Manchester United.

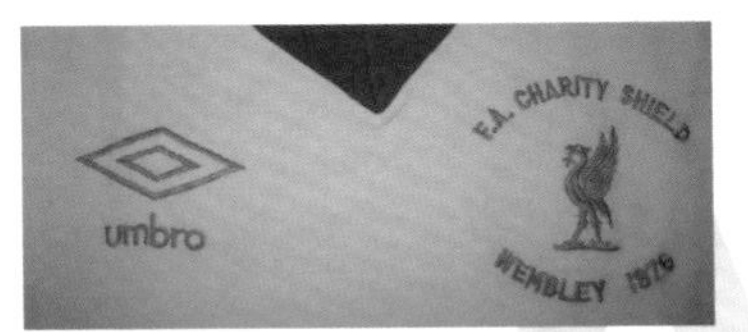

FA Charity Shield '76 &'77

1977-78 Team picture

TWO COLOURS CLEM

Ray Clemence's usual green jersey was replaced due to a colour clash by a temporary yellow version (made by adidas) for the 1977 European Cup quarter-final against St Etienne (bottom).

ROC4 OIL ROC4 OIL
ROC4 OIL

1978-1979

Rampant Reds gain Forest revenge

1978-1979

KIT DESIGN Umbro

78/79 PLAYERS David Johnson, Phil Neal, Alan Kennedy

MANAGER Bob Paisley

ABOUT THE KIT

Liverpool used an official third strip for the first time during the campaign – certainly in the FA Cup semi-final against Manchester United, and at Southampton in April 1979 (see picture, right). The kit was all yellow (with no colour contrast on collar or cuffs) with red logos. It was also never made available as a replica. Incidentally the Umbro logo on the shirt became less prominent and it was to be the final season the Liverpool kit was worn in every game without a shirt sponsor.

v Southampton, April 1979

Third strip

ON-FIELD

Having finished as runners-up to rivals Nottingham Forest the previous season, Liverpool reversed the trend in style, claiming their 11th Championship by eight points, being unbeaten at Anfield and dropping only two points at home in the process (via two draws - it was still two points for a win). It was also revenge for defeat to Brian Clough's side in the first round of the European Cup, the champions and European Cup holders being unfortunate enough to draw each other early on.

It was a relatively poor season in the cups, with a shock first-round exit also coming in the League Cup to Sheffield United, while Anderlecht edged a two-legged European Super Cup.

Paisley's men improved somewhat in the FA Cup, the Reds' Double dreams only being extinguished in the semi-finals against Manchester United in a replay at Goodison Park.

Home kit

'78 League Cup kit

OFF-FIELD

Following the shock League Cup defeat to Sheffield United in August, the Reds met Tottenham Hotspur at Anfield who included Argentine World Cup winners Osvaldo Ardilles and Ricky Villa in their side. Clearly smarting from that defeat though, any thoughts that Spurs could win at Liverpool for the first time in 1912 were soon extinguished as Bob Paisley's men ran in seven goals without reply, dishing out the Londoners' heaviest-ever league defeat. Indeed, of Terry McDermott's goal which made it 7-0, Paisley was quoted thus: "That must be the best goal that Anfield has ever seen."

FAMOUS MATCH
Liverpool 7-0 Tottenham H. (Division One).

UMBRO AUTHENTICITY (1)

Original shirt label taken from the home shirt.

UMBRO AUTHENTICITY (2)

Marking included on a bottom corner of the white away top.

DID YOU KNOW?

The 68-point total (2 points for a win) achieved in winning the title was a new club and First Division record. Only four league matches were lost, while only Leeds United and Everton escaped from Anfield with a point.
One newspaper rewarded the club for achieving an average of two goals per league game, confirmed in the last match at Leeds.

White shirt

MINOR DETAILS

The regular away shirt during the 1970s changed little, with a simple white and red collar complemented by sportswear logo and LFC badge. However, Kenny Dalglish is pictured above in a slightly different shirt during 78-79 at Arsenal (as were the players in the away kit shown in the lead in to this section), with no Umbro writing below the logo - while these are in red, and not yellow/gold as shown in the shirt (left).

NO LOGO

The final season of non-sponsorship, before Hitachi came on board. Indeed that would be the only change made to the kit the next season.

1979-1981

Plasters in Paris

1979-1981

KIT DESIGN Umbro /// **KIT SPONSOR** Hitachi

79/81 PLAYERS Phil Thompson, Graeme Souness
MANAGER Bob Paisley

HITACHI

ABOUT THE KIT

Liverpool became the first professional club to feature a sponsor's logo on their shirts for the 1979-80 season (the kit remained unchanged apart from the sponsor's addition). Derby County had signed a deal with Saab in 1977-1978, but the logo never appeared in competitive matches, only on shirts as part of the sponsorship deal. The name on the shirt was limited in size by the Football League (a two-and-a-half inch strip) in order to placate fans and the 'non advertising' BBC. Some products, such as cigarettes were considered unsuitable, although alcohol products, as today, featured. Both the BBC and ITV refused to broadcast matches featuring branded shirts, which forced clubs to remove the logos when the cameras were present. Shirt advertising was also not permitted for FA Cup ties or European games. This rule meant that the deal was worth only at least a fifth of what the club could possibly have received from shirt sponsorship at this time (the Hitachi deal yielded £50,000 over 12 months).

The yellow third kit, used from at least 1979 in that year's FA Cup semi-final against Manchester United was worn in the 2-2 draw against Southampton at The Dell in September 1980 (see Phil Neal picture on page 115), although a yellow with red pinstripes shirt was also introduced around this period.

Another change in this season was to the sponsor's lettering, which became bolder on all kits.

'81 League Cup final

Home shirt

ON-FIELD

Bob Paisley maintained Liverpool's success during these two seasons, retaining the First Division title in 1980 ahead of Manchester United, and like the previous 1978-79 season, Aston Villa were beaten in the decisive game. However, the Reds were beaten in the FA Cup semi-finals in a replay for a second successive season, this time by Arsenal.

As well as two more FA Charity Shield triumphs in 1979 and 1980, the first of four successive League Cups (by then sponsored by the Milk Marketing Board and known as the `Milk Cup') was claimed in 1981 - while memorably a third European Cup was secured, Real Madrid going down 1-0 to an Alan Kennedy strike in Paris in May. Ironically that season saw Liverpool slump to 5th in the table - their lowest First Division finish in 10 years.

White and yellow change tops

OFF-FIELD

It was Kettering Town who first wore a sponsor's name on their shirts ('Kettering Tyres') for a Southern League game in January 1976. However, this strip did not get another run-out as the FA ordered the club to remove the name. They did continue for a few months wearing the slogan `Kettering T' as club chief executive Derek Dougan claimed the 1972 FA ban on sponsorship had not been put down in writing. However the threat of a hefty fine proved too much and the new slogan was removed.

Away top

FAMOUS MATCH

Liverpool 1-0 Real Madrid (European Cup final).

'81 EUROPEAN CUP LOGO

Umbro's failure to contribute money to the collective UEFA sponsorship fund meant that the logo on Liverpool's shirt and shorts was covered (see below). However, as was customary in major finals, the Reds were allowed to display a special badge, as highlighted (right).

THE LIVER BIRD

Selected crests taken from the kits of the time.

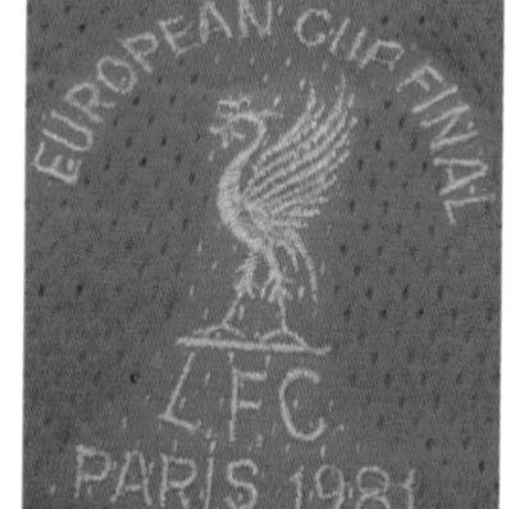

DID YOU KNOW?

A certain youngster by the name of Ian Rush made his first-team debut for Liverpool following his transfer from Chester City the previous season, wearing the unfamiliar No 7 shirt at Ipswich Town in December, 1980.

Liverpool's first game in a sponsored strip was against Borussia Moenchengladbach in a pre-season friendly in Germany – the Reds won 4-2.

All yellow away

Clem's '81 jersey

GOALKEEPER KIT

The pictures show Ray Clemence's 1981 European Cup-winning jersey, which can be viewed at the club museum.

'81 European Cup (left)

UMBRO/HITACHI KIT LAUNCH

Phil Thompson posed in the new Liverpool shirt with model Toni Byrne in July 1979. The photographs were taken on the site of what is now Clayton Square in the centre of Liverpool, with the red shirt sporting a 'name' for the first time following the club's signing of a one-year deal with Japanese electrical giants Hitachi. The press generally accepted shirt sponsorship although at the time it was assumed that only the Reds and Manchester United could attract sponsors.

HITACHI

LEAGUE CUP '81

A variation to the European Cup final badge logo later in the season, the League Cup final design worn on the shirt followed the pattern used in the European Cup triumph of 1977.

1981-1982

World first and the death of a legend

1981-1982

KIT DESIGN Umbro /// **KIT SPONSOR** Hitachi

81/82 PLAYERS Mark Lawrenson, Ronnie Whelan

MANAGER Bob Paisley

HITACHI

Away top

ABOUT THE KIT

Although the home strip again remained unchanged, a new all-yellow strip was officially introduced incorporating red pinstripes (front and back), red cuffs and a V-shaped neck and collar. The yellow shorts and socks included a red diamond trim. It was also to be the last season of Hitachi's kit sponsorship, the sponsor's logo permitted on shirts for domestic non-televised games only.

ON-FIELD

After the domestic disappointment of a 'lowly' fifth-place finish the season before, the Reds recovered their First Division form to claim the Championship ahead of Ipswich Town. The League Cup was also retained by the Reds, a 3-1 victory over Tottenham Hotspur achieved after extra time with Liverpool forcing the added 30 minutes courtesy of an equaliser by Ronnie Whelan three minutes from time.
As reigning European champions, the club were invited to face South American champions Flamengo in the World Club Championship. However, the Brazilians, inspired by Zico, proved a cut above on the day, claiming a 3-0 triumph.
In the other competitions entered that season, there were defeats to CSKA Sofia in round three of the European Cup, and to Chelsea in the fifth round of the FA Cup.

OFF-FIELD

The death of Bill Shankly cast a dark shadow over the club, the man who made Liverpool great passing away on September 29, 1981. There were emotional scenes before the European Cup tie against Oulu Palloseura the following day, the first match played at Anfield following his death. There were similar scenes before the first League game the following Saturday against Swansea City, whose manager John Toshack wore a red Liverpool shirt under his tracksuit top as a salute to the man who brought him to Anfield as a player.

Home with and without sponsor

FAMOUS MATCH

Liverpool 2-2 Swansea City (First Division).

CLASSIC LIVER BIRD

The classic Liverpool badge, completed with simple Liver bird and 'L.F.C.' legend.

REDS' SPONSOR

It was to be the final season of Hitachi on the home and away shirts, with these logos taken from two shirts during the campaign.

DID YOU KNOW?

Three points for a win were introduced by the Football League.

The 1981 World Club Championship saw favourites Liverpool beaten 3-0 by Flamengo in Tokyo, inspired by playmaker Zico. At the request of the Japanese organisers, both teams wore names on the back of their shirts. Tickets are worth around £100 for this game and programmes £60-£80.

3rd shirt

Alan Kennedy's shirt from the World Club Championship (pictured in the club museum) was the traditional all-red strip, with Flamengo playing in white shirts and shorts (with red sleeves on the shirt), completed by red and black-striped socks. As well as playing in a shirt without the 'Hitachi' logo, kit manufacturers 'Umbro' were unable to display their legend, instead having to make do with just the Umbro diamond more prominent in the 1970s.

Away (no sponsor)

'81 World Club final

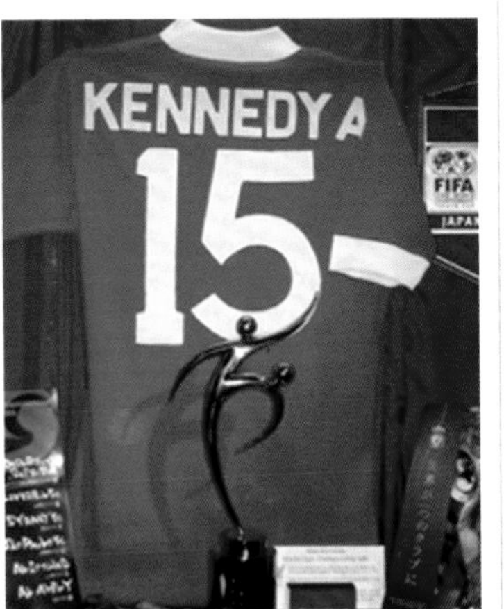

1982-1984

Same kit, same success

1982-1984

KIT DESIGN Umbro /// KIT SPONSOR Crown Paints

82/84 PLAYERS Ian Rush, Alan Hansen, Gary Gillespie

MANAGERS Bob Paisley, Joe Fagan

CROWN PAINTS

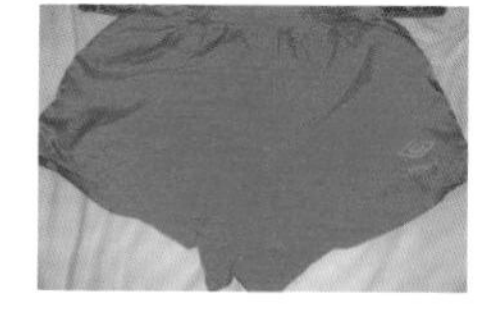

ABOUT THE KIT

The onset of the 1982-83 campaign saw the introduction of a new home strip for the first time since the mid-1970s, and a real change in design. Like the previous season's yellow away strip, fashionable pinstripes were incorporated but only on the front of the shirt, in white. A white band ran down the sides of the red shorts, with a white diamond band around the tops of the red socks.

There was also a change in kit sponsor, although like with Hitachi, the 'Crown Paints' logo was not allowed to be worn when the club's games were televised for the 1982-83 season.

Home kit

ON-FIELD

Entering the period as defending champions, Liverpool completed a remarkable three successive titles by claiming the First Division in 1983 and 1984. In addition, a League Cup 'treble' was completed courtesy of another two League Cup successes (1983, 1984), while there was also an FA Charity Shield win in 1982 over Tottenham Hotspur. The highlight though, was a fourth European Cup success, this time over AS Roma in their own stadium in 1984. The penalty shoot-out triumph following a 1-1 draw was best encapsulated by Bruce Grobbelaar's 'spaghetti legs' routine which helped unsettle the Italians and provide inspiration for another triumph over 20 years later. The team's success during 1982-1984 came about too during a relative period of upheaval, with Bob Paisley's retirement in 1983, with Joe Fagan taking over for the following season. But the changeover was seamless, and the Reds' first-ever treble followed.

Phil Thompson testimonial

Home top (no sponsor)

OFF-FIELD

Bob Paisley stepped down at the end of the 1982-83 season, ending a nine-season spell where he eclipsed the legendary Shankly to become the most successful manager in the club's history. His record stands at: 6 League titles, 3 League Cups, 3 European Cups, 1 UEFA Cup, 1 European Super Cup and 3 Charity Shields (2 shared).

'84 European Cup

FAMOUS MATCH

Liverpool 1-1 AS Roma (1984 European Cup final).

STITCHED ON

This picture shows preparations underway on the 1984 European Cup final shirt.

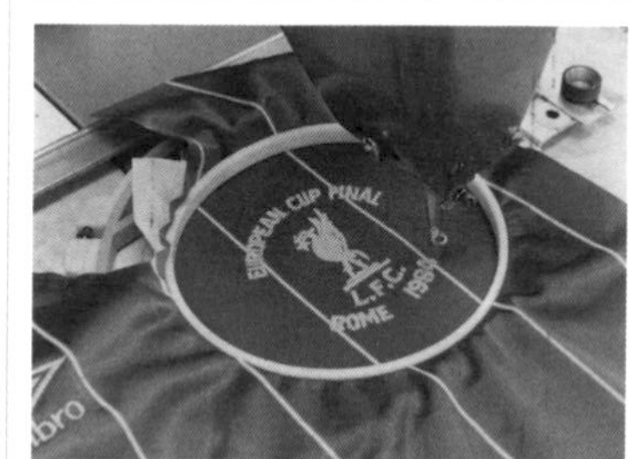

CLASSIC LFC LOGO

The classic, completed design of the '84 Rome shirt.

DID YOU KNOW?

1983 saw TV companies relent in their stance towards shirt sponsorship. The BBC and ITV allowed clubs to wear kit sponsorship, which immediately sent the value of potential deals for clubs more likely to feature on television (mainly the bigger, top-flight clubs) to rise steeply – certainly for the era. However, Football League regulations restricted the size of logos

Away shirts 82-84

SHIRT CHANGES

Due to TV regulations involving shirt sponsorship (see 'Did You Know'), the 'Crown Paints' logo appeared in different guises on the home and away shirts during the period. Two versions of the yellow shirt are shown (left), while Alan Hansen is in action wearing a home shirt from a game played away from the prying eyes of TV.

to a maximum of 81 square centimetres (32 square inches), while for televised games they had to be half this size. In Liverpool's case, the 'Crown Paints' logo usually took up 'two lines' on the shirt - but was squeezed onto one line for televised occasions.

The 1984 European Cup final programme is worth around £50, with a ticket valued at nearer the £40 mark.

When the league title, the League Cup and European Cup were secured in 1984, the Reds were the first English side to do the treble.

The 1984 European Cup penalty takers (Nicol, Rush, Neal, Souness, Kennedy) had a practice shoot-out with the younger players at Anfield in the build-up to the final with AS Roma - and lost 4-1!

Ian Rush's 47 goals in 83-84 remains a club record.

1984-1985

Runners-up and tragedy abroad

1984-1985

KIT DESIGN Umbro /// **KIT SPONSOR** Crown Paints

84/85 PLAYERS Paul Walsh, Michael Robinson

MANAGER Joe Fagan

CROWN PAINTS

ABOUT THE KIT

The final Liverpool Umbro home strip remained unchanged but the all-yellow change kit saw a new shirt and shorts introduced. Officially titled 'World Cup', yellow pinstripes were added to the red collar and cuffs with the developments in kit technology meaning that the material was now ribbed, giving the shirt a two-tone effect. The shorts were similar to the previous two seasons, apart from the addition of a red stripe down the sides, while the socks were the same as used on the previous yellow away strip – yellow with a red Umbro band on the turn-ups.

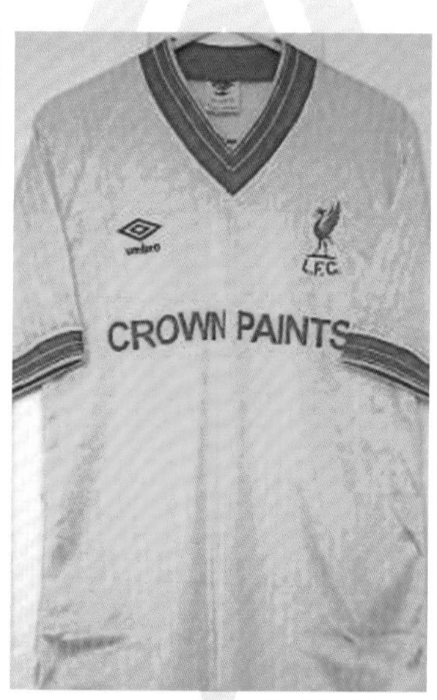

84-85 away

ON-FIELD

After the treble success of the previous campaign, 1984-85 proved a season of near misses for Joe Fagan's men. Beginning with defeat to Everton in the FA Charity Shield, the Reds went out to Tottenham Hotspur in round three of the League Cup and in December, lost 1-0 to Argentinian giants Independiente in the World Club Championship.

A month later Juventus claimed the European Super Cup, defeating the Reds 2-0 in Italy and hopes of FA Cup success were also ended at the semi-final stage, Manchester United edging through in a replay.

In the First Division the Reds paid for inconsistency in the first half of the season, finally recovering to finish as runners-up behind Everton. However, the European Cup holders did reach the final again, although the 1-0 defeat to Juventus meant little in relation to the tragedy that occurred before the final in Brussels.

World Club Championship, 1984

OFF-FIELD

The European Cup final of 1985 against Juventus was overshadowed by a riot between boths sets of supporters before the match. The inadequacy of the Heysel Stadium in Brussels, together with the violence culminated in a crush on the terraces and a wall giving way. 39 people died, although the final still took place, the theory being that to cancel the final at the last minute may create more chaos. It proved to be manager Joe Fagan's last match before retirement.

FAMOUS MATCH
Liverpool 4-0 Panathinaikos (European Cup semi-final).

LAST UMBRO LOGO

The diamond logo was a regular feature of the red shirt during the 70s and 80s. This was the last worn on the red shirt, complete with 'small' lettering.

CHARITY SHIELD '84

The FA Charity Shield was not deemed an occasion worth creating a special shirt for during the period – hence the usual home strip here.

DID YOU KNOW?

Paul Walsh scored after only 14 seconds of his Anfield debut in the 3-0 defeat of West Ham United in August, 1984.

Kenny Dalglish was sent off for the first time in his career at Benfica in the European Cup.

The 1984 World Club Championship programme and ticket stub are worth up to £100 each.

84-85 home

CHANGE STRIP

When a kit clash occurred with the home team's shorts and/or socks, the away shorts or socks were often used. In this case, and with Liverpool's away yellow shirts clashing with Watford's home strip, training shorts and away socks were used. Note too the plain 'No 4' of Mark Lawrenson – a style that was soon to change once adidas took over the kit sponsorship.

Collection

1985-1987

Crown Paints, Cup finals and Kenny Dalglish

1985-1987

KIT DESIGN adidas /// KIT SPONSOR Crown Paints

85-87 PLAYERS Steve McMahon, Craig Johnston

PLAYER-MANAGER Kenny Dalglish

crown paints

ABOUT THE KIT

The change from Umbro to adidas saw an inauspicious start, with the strip (worn without a kit sponsor or 'adidas' lettering) being first worn for the 1985 European Cup final. The traditional all-red home strip was retained (although a more tighter fit), with the addition of white adidas stripes (first used on clothing in 1967) on the shoulders (with a yellow trim) - but not the sleeves.

The shirt, which incorporated a V-neck, also included faint lines within the design within which were rows of Liver birds and adidas 'leaves' in the material. The white adidas lines were included on the shorts and the sock tops. The adidas and Liver bird logos were included on the shirt (along with the Crown Paints kit sponsor) and shorts - and were in white rather than the gold/yellow that had been prominent until the early 1970s. Only the famous adidas 'leaves' were included in the middle of the socks.

The traditional white and black away strip was revived, the kit mirroring the home design. It was a white shirt with red and yellow trim, black or white shorts with white or red and yellow trim (although red shorts were also used dependent on kit clashes) and white socks with red and yellow trim (or the home red socks).

For the first time a third strip was also officially launched - although it was rarely used. It was exactly the same only in all yellow, with the logos in red.

'85 European Cup top

Home shirts

ON-FIELD

1985-86 saw Liverpool do the League and FA Cup Double – pipping Everton to both honours in the process. The Screen Sport Super Cup was introduced for English clubs who had qualified for Europe but could not compete due to a UEFA ban (see below). Liverpool were the first and only winners, securing the trophy in 1986-87 after the competition was held over from the previous season – beating Everton in the final over two legs. Incidentally the Reds shared the FA Charity Shield with the Blues in August 1986, although they lost the League Cup final to Arsenal later that campaign wearing the 'third' kit.

Special edition shirt

'Away' socks

OFF-FIELD

Due to escalating English hooliganism abroad which culminated in the disorder at Heysel before the 1985 European Cup final, English clubs were banned from European competition for an indefinite period (which was later lifted and ran until the 1990-91 season).

Yellow away strip

FAMOUS MATCH
Liverpool 3–1 Everton (1986 FA Cup final).

NUMBERS ON BACK

This example is taken from the home shirt.

EMBROIDERED SHIRTS

Special edition logos from the 1986–87 campaign.

DID YOU KNOW?

When the team were shown on television, the usual 'Crown Paints' logo had to be worn on one line rather than the usual two.
Liverpool's Double success in 1986 was only the third-ever achieved in English football.
The 1987 League final was the first competitive game in which Ian Rush had scored and been on the losing team for the Reds.

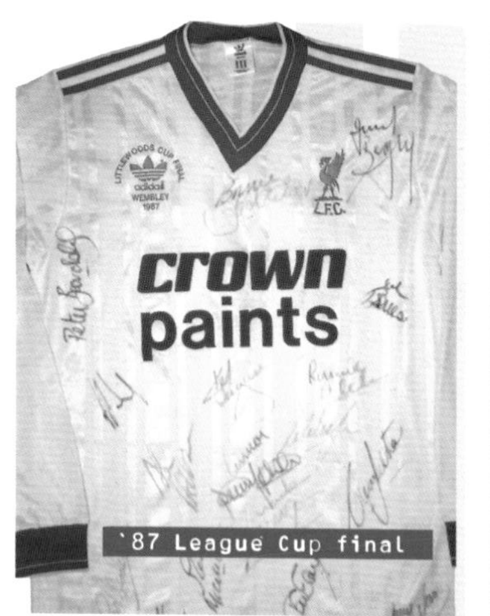

'87 League Cup final

Home shorts and socks

GOALKEEPER KIT

Although the green version (below, top) was worn in the 1986 FA Cup final, a yellow shirt was more commonly used by Bruce Grobbelaar and No 2 Mike Hooper. Introduced in 1985-86, it is one of the first examples of Liverpool having two different keeper tops.

Third kit

THE OUTFIELD RANGE

Due to the availability of shirts from this period owned by a variety of sources including collectors like Colin Wright, we felt it only fair to showcase some of the shirts from the first two seasons of Liverpool's shirt sponsorship deal with adidas. The opportunity to highlight the special edition 'Double' away shirt was also too good to miss. Incidentally it is claimed that this version was only worn twice, including once in a pre-season friendly in Ireland.

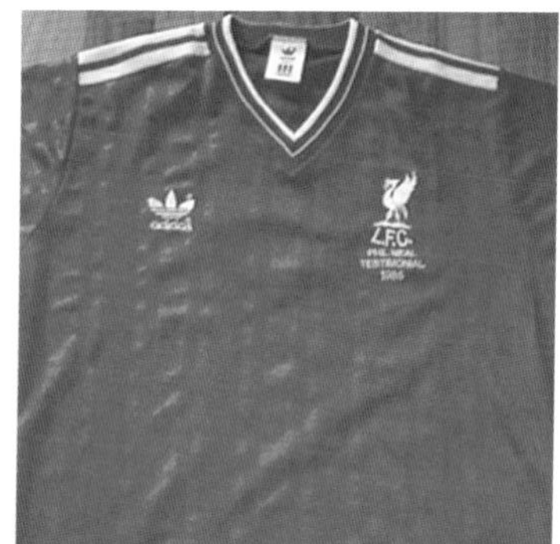

Phil Neal testimonial

85-87 away

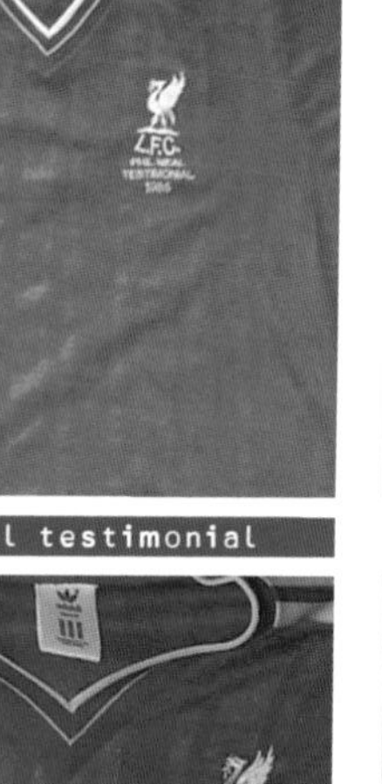

Sammy Lee testimonial

85-87 away (back)

85-88 away/3rd shirt

`86 FA Cup final

`85 European Cup logo

`87 League Cup kit

crown

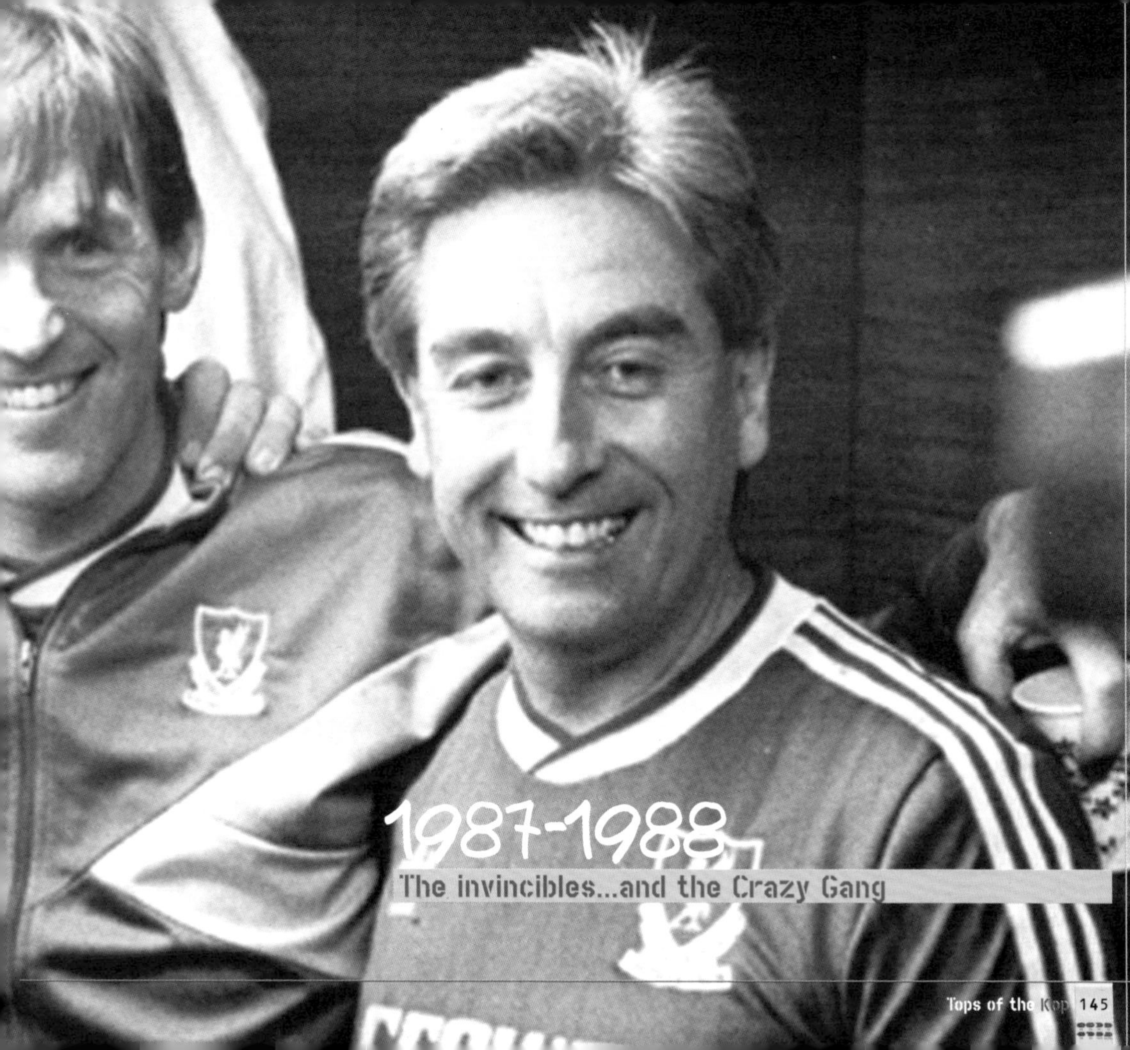

1987-1988

The invincibles...and the Crazy Gang

1987-1988

KIT DESIGN adidas /// **KIT SPONSOR** Crown Paints

87-88 PLAYERS John Barnes, Steve Nicol, Gary Ablett
PLAYER-MANAGER Kenny Dalglish

crown paints

ABOUT THE KIT

New home, away and third kits were launched. The classic all red home saw the return of the round neck white collar while the three white stripes were extended right down the sleeves, giving it a classic adidas look. Up close you could also distinguish horizontal panels bearing the Liver bird and adidas logo. The hint of yellow on the previous home strip was now removed completely – to be replaced by silver/grey trim. The badge also changed, with the traditional Liver bird on both shirt and shorts now sitting inside a crest – which wasn't a popular choice wih everyone.

The shorts included the familiar three white stripes down the sides, with the white stripes also on the sock turn-ups – with an adidas logo centred in the socks.
This was also the season when the silver/grey away kit was introduced, an ambitious but successful leap from the traditional whites and yellows of the past. It retained the same design as the home version. In the event, two away strips had to be produced after the initial white sponsor with red trim was replaced with solid red letters so it could be seen better.

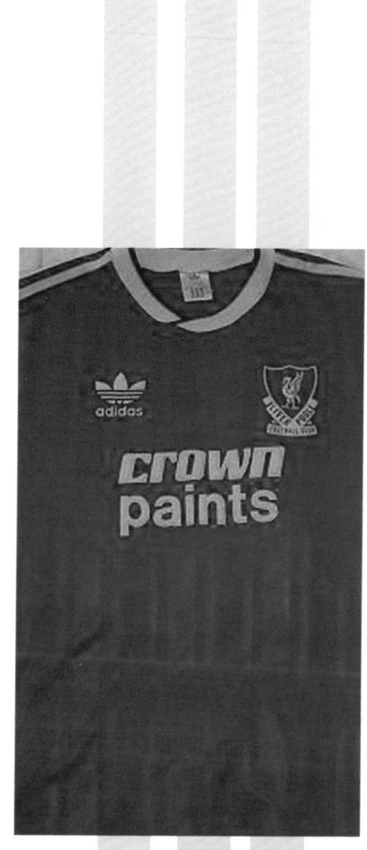

Home kit

ON-FIELD

If ever a Liverpool side deserved to win the Double then it was this one – and how they didn't remains a mystery. Beaten only twice in the League all season, it took neighbours Everton to inflict a first defeat which ended the Reds' hopes of setting a new unbeaten record of 30 games from the start of the season. Overall they suffered only four defeats, never by more than one goal. In the League Cup Everton knocked the Reds out 1-0 in round three courtesy of a late deflected Gary Stevens goal, while dreams of a second Double in three seasons were dashed by underdogs Wimbledon courtesy of a Lawrie Sanchez header in the FA Cup final at Wembley. It was a day to forget, as Peter Beardsley saw a good goal disallowed when the referee refused to play the advantage rule, before John Aldridge saw a penalty saved by Dave Beasant. As BBC commentator John Motson proclaimed at the final whistle: "The Crazy Gang have beaten the Culture Club."

OFF-FIELD

The 5-0 demolition of Nottingham Forest in April was described as one of the finest performances of all time, with some claiming that the Brazil side of any era would have come off second best to the Reds that night.

New colour...

One of England's finest -ever players, Tom Finney, described it thus: "Liverpool must be the best team of all time. It was the finest exhibition I have seen by a team in all my time of playing and watching the game."

FAMOUS MATCH

Liverpool 5-0 Nottingham Forest (Division 1).

WHITE SPONSOR

A rare sighting on the grey/silver away strip, the 'crown paints' sponsor was changed to red to make it more prominent.

CUP FINAL SHIRT

Like previous finals when adidas sponsored the kit, it would be around the sportswear manufacturer's logo where the commemorative Cup final message was written on the shirt.

DID YOU KNOW?

It was a record-breaking season for the Reds. In winning the League title for a 17th time, the club recorded a record points total (90 from 40 games), lost only 2 games (a then record) and equalled Leeds United's record of going the first 29 games of a season unbeaten (a run of 31 games taking in the previous season). John Aldridge also set a club record by scoring

Signed cup final shirt

in 10 successive league games.
When Dave Beasant saved John Aldridge's penalty in the FA Cup final, it was the first spot-kick to be saved at Wembley in a major Cup final. The programme from this final is valued at around £2, with a ticket worth double.

Aldo's No 8

THIRD CHOICE

Despite no obvious clash with the silver/grey away strip, this kit (below) was worn by the Reds at Aston Villa in the FA Cup fourth-round tie of January 1988. Utilising the home shorts and socks, the shirt was the white worn as an away colour in the previous two seasons – including the 1987 League Cup final. Relegated to third choice, it still did the trick as Liverpool won a tricky encounter 2-0.

NEC
Candy
Candy
NEC
SMIRNOFF
SMIRNOFF

1988–1989

Tragedy and triumph

1988-1989

KIT DESIGN adidas /// **KIT SPONSOR** Candy

88-89 PLAYERS Ray Houghton, John Aldridge

PLAYER-MANAGER Kenny Dalglish

crown paints

Third top

ABOUT THE KIT

Despite the home and away strips remaining unchanged from the classic kit of the previous season, there was one major change being in the change of kit sponsor to `Candy', the third name to appear on the Liverpool shirts. A new third shirt was also used during the campaign, similar to the previous white shirt. Again sported in a game at Aston Villa, it was a replica of the silver/grey away kit but in white, with red and silver/grey trim. The home shorts and socks were also used. A replica was never released.

Home kit

ON-FIELD

With the First Division having reverted to 20 teams (the previous season, for one season only, it had 21 teams), the Reds led Arsenal by three points going into their rearranged last game of the season – against the Gunners. The Reds had already won the FA Cup, beating Everton in a dramatic final 3-2 after extra time, after the Toffees had twice levelled, the first time in the last minute of normal time.

Liverpool could take the title for a second successive season and claim their second Double in four seasons – as long as they avoided a two-goal defeat.

Unfortunately a disputed Alan Smith goal in the second half, and then Michael Thomas – who would later join the club – in the last seconds, stunned Anfield and snatched the title for George Graham's men.

Other action had seen the club gain revenge on Wimbledon for the FA Cup defeat the previous season in the FA Charity Shield, winning 2-1 while West Ham inflicted a League Cup loss in round four.

Away front and back

OFF-FIELD

15th April, 1989 will always be linked with the Hillsborough disaster. A total of 96 Liverpool fans died at the FA Cup semi-final against Nottingham Forest, crushed at the Leppings Lane end of the ground. Football would be changed forever, with fans' safety suddenly lifted to the top of the agenda. The resulting Taylor Report would recommend all-seater stadiums, and despite protests, signalled the end of the famous Kop terrace five years later.

FAMOUS MATCH

Liverpool 3–2 Everton (FA Cup final).

FA CUP FINAL LOGO

Taken from a 1989 final original, a simple 'legend' accompanied the usual LFC crest. The year before it had been written around the adidas logo.

TRADITIONAL ADIDAS

A regular addition to the red shirt during the period, the traditional three-leaf logo.

DID YOU KNOW?

The agonising defeat to Arsenal in the final game of the season at Anfield cost Liverpool the Championship. To date it is the closest top-flight title race ever.
Programme and ticket valuations (estimates) for the period are:
1988 FA Charity Shield – £15 programme, half that for ticket.
1989 FA Cup final – £10 programme, ticket £7.

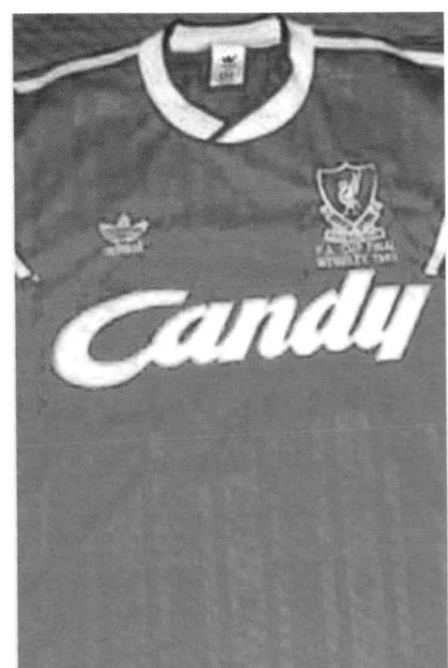

PLAIN GREEN

Mirroring the simple design of the home strip, the goalkeeper's jersey was light green with the only variation being a plain white rounded collar with small lapel.

FA Cup final '89

Candy

1989-1991

The end of an era

1989-1991

KIT DESIGN adidas /// **KIT SPONSOR** Candy

89-91 PLAYERS Glenn Hysen, Ronny Rosenthal

MANAGERS Kenny Dalglish, Graeme Souness

Home shirt

ABOUT THE KIT

Liverpool's new home and away strip, launched ahead of the 1989-90 season, signalled a more modern design for the era which included a baggier shirt than in previous years. It reflected fashions around the period of loud clothing full of shapes and angles.

The all-red home strip included light red and white flashes (a major shift from the plain red shirt synonymous with the club), the usual three white stripes on the shoulders and arms and the same round neck. The shorts were also altered to include three red stripes down the sides on a thick white strip, while the socks also included adidas' three stripes (in red) on the white turn-ups. The away kit was the last to be produced in silver/grey and came with contrasting diamond shades running diagonally across the shirt – while the adidas 'touches' were in red. Quoted in 2002, Steven Gerrard voted it his least favourite: "The one with all the speckles on it, that was bad."

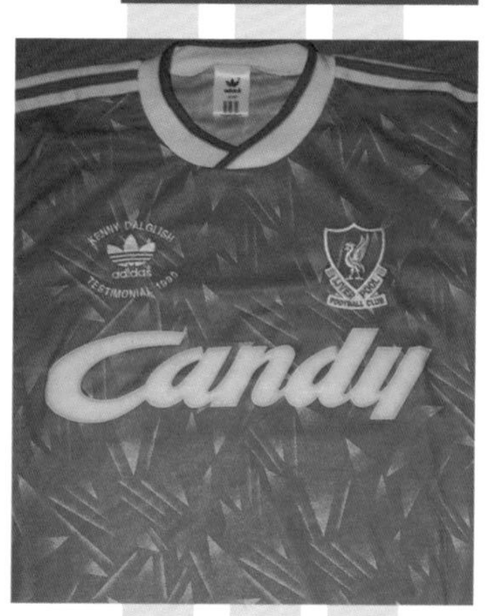

Kenny testimonial top

ON-FIELD

The period included the club's last Championship triumph (1990) to date, and the collection of more silverware underneath the Twin Towers (FA Charity Shield winners in 1989, sharing it a year later). Following the agonising last-day title setback against Arsenal in 1988-89, the Reds hit back to storm to the title - their record 18th success. A season later the Reds were runners-up, with Arsenal taking the Championship, losing only one game in the process. However, it did secure a return to European competition.

The semi-finals of the FA Cup were the furthest the club reached in the cup competitions in these two seasons, being stunned 4-3 by Crystal Palace at Villa Park in 1990 - this in the same season that the Reds demolished them at Anfield (see 'Did You Know').

The following season and following a stunning 4-4 FA Cup fifth-round replay draw at Everton, Kenny Dalglish would resign. The Reds would also lose the third game 1-0.

Sample shirt number

OFF-FIELD

Player-manager Kenny Dalglish retired from outfield duties at the end of the 1989-90 season. He remains the only player to score 100 goals in the Scottish and English leagues and was capped 102 times by his country.

The following season he would resign, citing the pressures of the job, to be replaced by Graeme Souness in April 1991.

UEFA confirmed that English clubs would be allowed back in European competition for the 1990-91 season. League runners-up Aston Villa were allocated a UEFA Cup place and FA Cup winners Manchester United were handed a spot in the European Cup Winners' Cup - although champions Liverpool were not permitted for another season.

FAMOUS MATCH

Everton 4-4 Liverpool (FA Cup).

KENNY'S GAME

Logo worn for Kenny Dalglish's testimonial match.

CLUB BADGE

The crests as seen on the club's home and away shirts.

DID YOU KNOW?

Crystal Palace shocked Liverpool in the FA Cup semi-final of 1990, winning 4-3 after extra time at Villa Park. Ironically earlier in that season the Reds had embarrassed the Londoners 9-0 at Anfield, in what proved to be John Aldridge's final game for the club (it is also the club's biggest-ever league win). 1990 was the last time the Reds won the league title, an

Away shirt

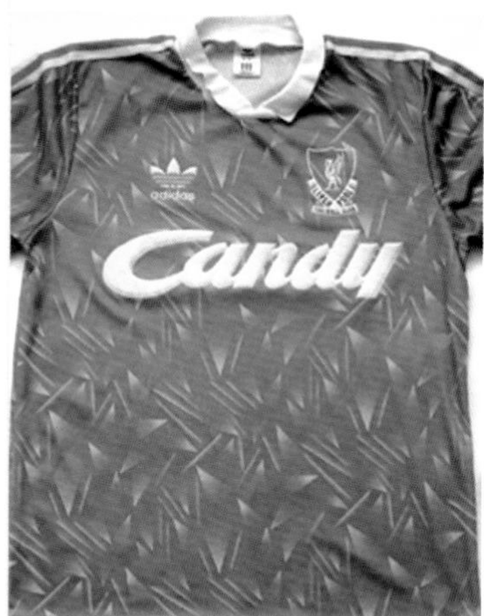

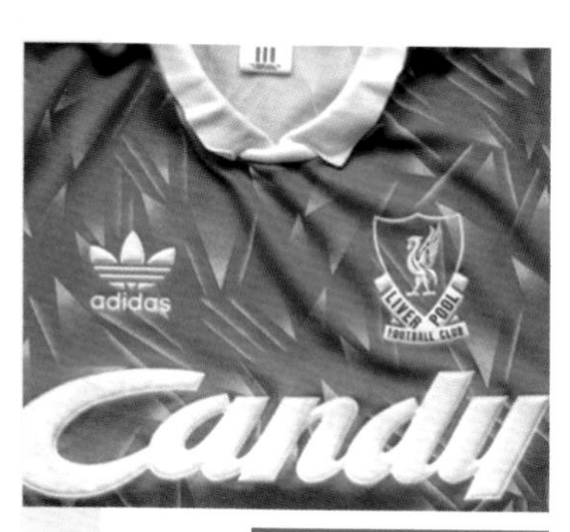

Keeper shirt

18th Championship success (a record). The last home game of this season against Derby County also saw a substitute appearance from player-manager Kenny Dalglish – his last game for the Reds.
Programme and ticket valuations: 1989 FA Charity Shield (£5 for each); 1990 FA Charity Shield (up to £7 ticket, £10 programme).

GREEN AND WHITE

Retaining the style of the home strip, the goalkeeper's jersey was a lighter shade of green, whilst also incorporating the adidas touches – namely white flashes and three stripes across the shoulders and arms.

1991-1992

Ups and downs for Souey

1991-1992

KIT DESIGN adidas /// **KIT SPONSOR** Candy

91-92 PLAYERS Dean Saunders, Mark Wright

MANAGER Graeme Souness

ABOUT THE KIT

Fashion is subjective – with football kits being no exception. The three white stripes over the shoulder – a mark of the new 'adidas equipment' logo – appeared as a new and courageous venture, a style common on the continent at the time (at clubs such as Bayern Munich and Marseille). Gone were the days when Liverpool wore an all-red kit with a hint of white to compliment it.
It was also in this season that adidas introduced the bottle green away shirt (replicating the home shirt design), with white (or green) shorts (longer than previous kits for both home and away strips) and green socks. It is not certain why the unusual Liverpool away colour was introduced – although it was the coporate colour of Carlsberg, who were due to take over from Candy as kit sponsors the following season.
Incidentally, the club never won a game in this strip.
The other major change for either shirt from previous season was that the Candy logo was now designed into the material – not sewn on as before. The same applied for the adidas logo, which had changed in design and was now situated in the middle stripe on the shirts.
Incidentally, there was more than just the usual addition of a logo marking the achievement when the Reds reached the FA Cup final. The 'Candy' and adidas logos were now embossed, with the 'adidas' moved into the collar, while the three white stripes were now sewn on.

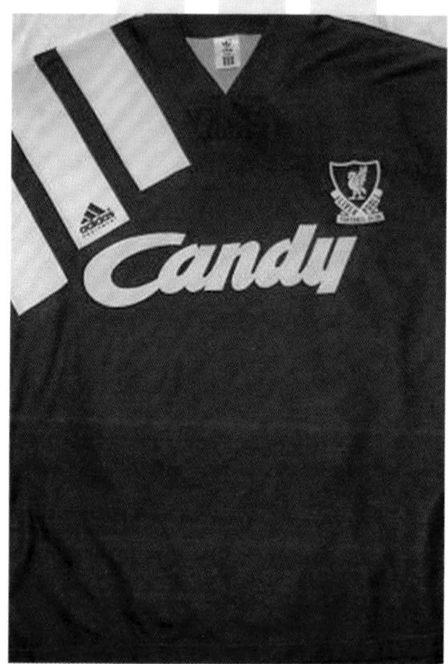

Away kit

ON-FIELD

After finishing as runners-up the previous season, the Reds dropped to 6th although the 2-0 defeat of Manchester United in their penultimate game of the season denied the Red Devils a first league title in 25 years.
The return to European competition in the UEFA Cup produced some remarkable encounters, including coming back from a two-goal first-leg deficit against French side Auxerre, but Genoa eventually proved too strong in round four, going through 4-1 on aggregate.
There was a shock in the League Cup, as Third Division Peterborough United became the first club from either of the basement leagues to defeat Liverpool in the competition, 1-0 at London Road.
However, the FA Cup success over Sunderland in 1992 at least rounded off a troubled season on a high note, as Graeme Souness, recently recovered from a heart bypass operation, witnessed a 2-0 victory at Wembley.

FA Cup '92 shirt

OFF-FIELD

The Reds beat off competition from Everton to secure the signature of Dean Saunders for a club record £2.9m. It was also the last season of the Football League First Division, the clubs having resigned and given their backing to a new FA Premier League, which in essence gave the clubs at the top more power - and more money (television monies were now shared out between clubs in the top flight only, rather than through all four divisions as before).
Phil Thompson was dismissed as reserve-team boss at the end of the season.

FAMOUS MATCH

Liverpool 2-0 Sunderland (FA Cup final).

LEAGUE LOGOS

Introduced the previous season, it was the final campaign where the Football League logo was prominent on the sleeves of the shirt.

WEMBLEY '92

The official logos worn on the goalkeeper's jersey (above) and the red shirt against Sunderland.

DID YOU KNOW?

Liverpool's 2-0 victory over Manchester United in April not only denied the Red Devils their first Championship since 1967 (it confirmed Leeds United as champions), but the first goal, scored by Ian Rush, was also the Welshman's first-ever goal against them.
No 2 Ronnie Moran led the Reds out at Wembley, with boss Graeme Souness having recently taken ill and been

STILL THE JOKER

Bruce Grobbelaar, who turned 34 during the campaign, played more games than anyone in the Liverpool squad in 1991-92, earning a third FA Cup winners' medal in the process.

Home shirt

Home shorts

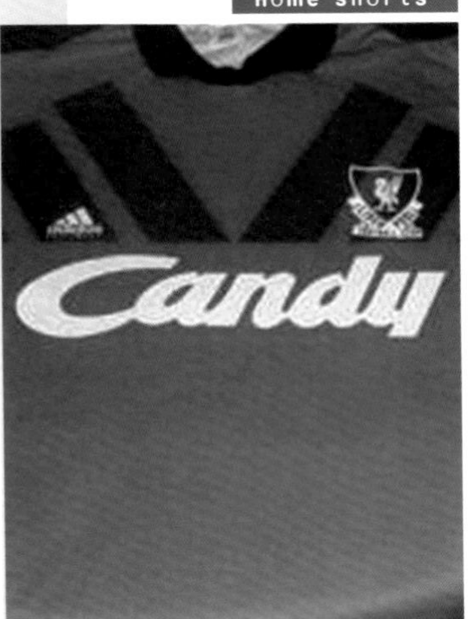

Keeper top

forced to undergo a heart bypass operation.
The club's sixth-place finish in the league was their lowest since finishing seventh in the 1964-65 season. Apart from in 1980-81, they had not finished lower than fifth.
The 1992 FA Cup final programme, issued with plastic key ring and large fold-out poster, is worth up to £50.

1992-1993

Premier inconsistency in centenary campaign

1992-1993

KIT DESIGN adidas /// **KIT SPONSOR** Carlsberg

92-93 PLAYERS Mark Walters, Paul Stewart

MANAGER Graeme Souness

ABOUT THE KIT

Although rumours were rife that a stick/iron transfer would be made available to put on the previous season's kit due to the change of kit sponsor, a new home and away strip were brought in to celebrate the Reds' centenary season. The kit design remained similar to the previous campaign, with three white stripes prominent on shirt and shorts while the socks remained similar, with red prominent and the sock tops white. It was also the first time the club badge was displayed on both home and away socks. The main change to the shirt was that the 'adidas equipment' logo was situated in the centre of the V-neck collar, while on the shorts this was in green. The logos and white stripes were also now all stitched on. The material was shinier and the home kit also took on a lighter shade of red than previous home strips. Another change saw a new badge displayed, this becoming more a shield design. The badge incorporated the Shankly Gates and the legends: 'You'll Never Walk Alone' and '100 years 1892-1992', with part of the badge green. It was the first time the colour had ever appeared on the home kit. Incidentally, the away strip remained green in keeping with the change brought in by adidas (with Carlsberg displayed proudly on the company corporate colour), with the logos in white.

Home kit

ON-FIELD

Although the Reds' centenary season began with a Wembley appearance in the FA Charity Shield (Leeds United winning 4-3), disappointing performances in the cup competitions, plus inconsistency in the first season of the FA Premier League meant that the season overall failed to live up to expectations.

Although the Reds finished 6th in the league for a second successive season, it was with a lower points tally. The Reds went out of the European Cup Winners' Cup in the second round, well beaten 6-2 on aggregate by Spartak Moscow, while a 2-1 fourth-round replay defeat to Crystal Palace ended Liverpool's participation in the League Cup. There was little to cheer in the FA Cup too, as Second Division Bolton Wanderers claimed victory in a third-round replay at Anfield, 2-0. It was declared the biggest cup shock the Reds had suffered since being beaten by Southern League Worcester City in 1959.

OFF-FIELD

The embarrassing cup exit to Bolton was also the first time Robbie Fowler had appeared on a Liverpool team sheet, as an unused substitute although he did not make his bow until the following season.

Home kit

FAMOUS MATCH

Man Utd 2-2 Liverpool (Premier League).

TRAINING TOP BADGE

Logo celebrating the club's centenary which appeared on 'club leisurewear'.

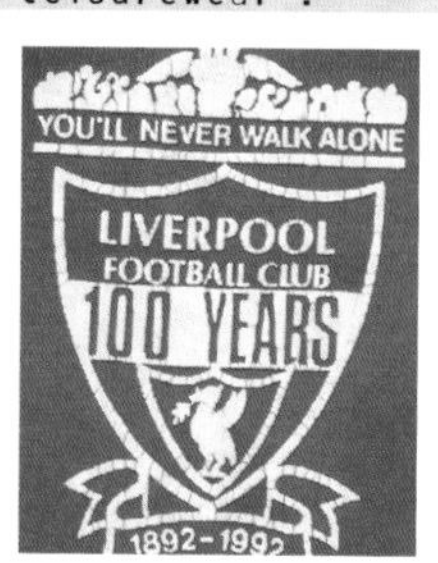

ADIDAS EQUIPMENT

Embroidered logo which improved on the 91-92 version.

DID YOU KNOW?

Ian Rush broke Roger Hunt's scoring record for the club, netting his 287th goal at Manchester United.

The 1993 League Cup final between Arsenal and Sheffield Wednesday was the first time names were worn on the back of shirts in an English club game.

Liverpool and Everton's FA Cup third-round exits was the first time both had gone out at that stage since 1951.

GREEN MEN

With green having been introduced into the Liverpool club colours by adidas the season before (replacing the grey/silver away colours), the sportswear manufacturer repeated the trick by introducing a similar strip for the away kit of 1992-93.

There was a subtle difference between players' kits and the replicas, with the players' shirts sporting an embroidered badge while the replica was ironed-on. These tops caused criticism as some shirts were uncomfortable and apparently caused chafing.

HOOPER MAN

A perennial second choice stopper during his Anfield career, Mike Hooper was an able understudy who made 15 appearances during the campaign. As well as this yellow version, there were also light green, and silver and black alternatives.

Man in yellow

Cola.
Coca-Cola.

1993-1995

Kop kids emerge

1993-1995

KIT DESIGN adidas /// **KIT SPONSOR** Carlsberg

93-95 PLAYERS Robbie Fowler, Rob Jones, Julian Dicks
MANAGERS Graeme Souness, Roy Evans

ABOUT THE KIT

In what would become common with the rise of commericalism in football, new home and away kits were again launched, which caused controversy at the time (due to the financial demands on parents to keep up with new kits). There was again a change to the badge, with the removal of the centenary legend, the Liver bird was made bigger and there was the addition of two torch flames either side of the shield, in memory of the 96 people who lost their lives at Hillsborough in 1989 (the badge was also moved, located in the middle of the shirt).
The material was of a greater quality than its predecessors, while the V-neck collar material was replicated on the cuffs (this was predominantly white, with thinner green and red stripes). There were also more white stripes on the shirt and shorts, with three 'adidas' stripes on either side of the shirt from hip level, rather than from the shoulders.
The away strip was in the same style, but was changed to white, green and black. The shirt was white with green sleeves, white cuffs and the adidas stripes in black. The shorts were black with white stripes and the socks were green with black tops and three white bands.
There was also an official third strip for only the second time ever, as worn at Sheffield United on Boxing Day 1993. The yellow shirt included black flecks, a button-up round collar and a type-only adidas logo, while the shorts and socks were black with yellow adidas stripes which came in a different design to the first two kits. The club had no plans to reproduce it, but such was the demand that it was in the shops the following summer.

League logo 93-95

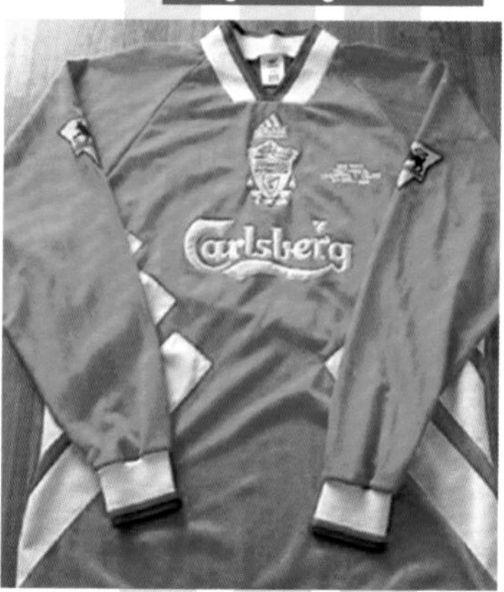

Shirt from Rush testimonial

ON-FIELD

The League Cup success of 1995, courtesy of a 2-1 victory over First Division Bolton Wanderers, ended a three-year trophy drought and signalled better times ahead. After finishing 8th in 1993-94, the Reds finished 4th the season after.
Without any European competition during the period, the FA Cup provided Liverpool's other opportunity for silverware but the year after the defeat to Bristol City in 1994 (see below) the Reds went out to a late goal in a 2-1 defeat to Tottenham Hotspur in the 1995 quarter-final.

OFF-FIELD

The 1994 FA Cup defeat to Bristol City was the final curtain for Graeme Souness, who was soon replaced by the final boot room graduate Roy Evans.
The new Kop was also officially opened in 1994.

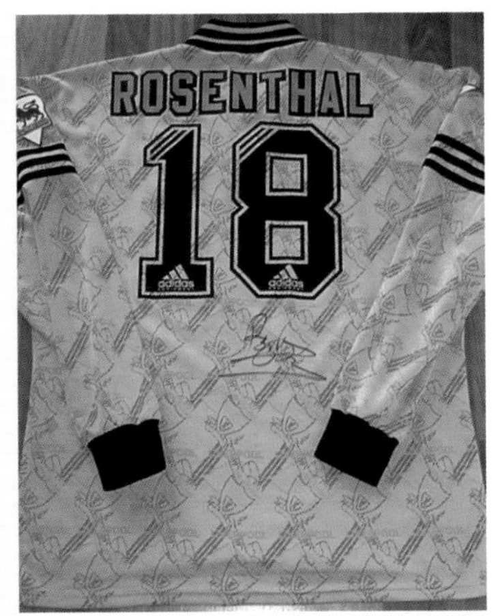

Away shirts

FAMOUS MATCH

Liverpool 3-3 Manchester United (Premier League).

WEMBLEY LOGO

Simple script added to the League Cup final badge.

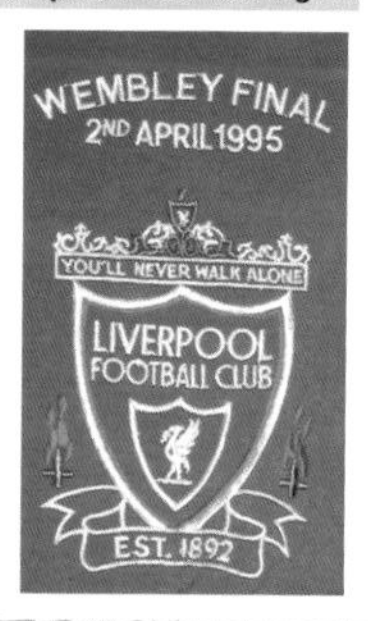

KEEPER TOP

One of two versions of the goalkeeper jersey.

DID YOU KNOW?

The 1993-94 season saw the introduction of squad numbers and players' names on the back of shirts. Bruce Grobbelaar was the first No 1 while the highest number to make a Premier League appearance (up to February 2007) is No 42, Nabil El Zhar. Robbie Fowler made a scoring first-team debut against Fulham in the League Cup, a 3-1 victory. In the return at Anfield he scored all five

Home top

goals in a 5-0 win – only the fourth player in the club's history to achieve that feat.
Liverpool's 8th-place finish was the club's worst in the top flight since 1962.
The penalty shoot-out defeat to Wimbledon in the League Cup is the club's only defeat by this method in 10 attempts.
April 30th, 1994 was the official goodbye to the standing Kop, a 1-0 defeat to Norwich City. Jeremy Goss was the goalscorer, while the last Liverpool player to score in front of the Kop was Julian Dicks.
Robbie Fowler's hat-trick against Arsenal in August, 1994 remains the quickest in Premiership history, timed at 4 minutes 35 seconds.
The 1995 League Cup programme is worth around £10, with an original ticket stub worth about half that.

HOME CHOICE

By now a home and away goalkeeper's kit was common for Liverpool teams. This 'web-like' creation, sported by David James, was an Anfield fixture during the period.

1995-1996

A legend bows out

1995-1996

KIT DESIGN adidas /// **KIT SPONSOR** Carlsberg

95-96 PLAYERS Stan Collymore, Neil Ruddock

MANAGER Roy Evans

ABOUT THE KIT

The last season of the club's deal with adidas saw two new strips brought in. The home shirt was a solid white V-neck with three white stripes down the shoulders and arms (incorporating yellow trimming) – the tradition returning after three years as `adidas equipment'. The collar, almost in the style of a traditional cricket jumper, also included a thin red stripe. The material was also part-perforated.
The shorts had three white stripes down either side , while the socks included three white stripes on the tops, with LFC/adidas written lower down. Another new badge was also introduced, a giant almost square crest that the club badge had been put in.
Green and white quarters were introduced to the away shirt, with the back becoming all white. It was a style steeped in Liverpool history as the club had started playing in a similar shirt – but in blue and white quarters or halves. Three black stripes were also introduced to the shoulders and sleeves, while the shirt now incorporated a white turtle-neck `Granddad-style' collar with buttons down the front. The green shorts included three white stripes down each side, while the white socks had three green stripes around the tops.

Home shirt

ON-FIELD

A season of what 'could have beens' as Liverpool missed out on a first FA Cup success in four years in the final against Manchester United thanks to a late Eric Cantona strike.

The Reds improved one place in the League to finish 3rd, although there was further disappointment in the other cup competitions. There was a shock second-round exit in the UEFA Cup, Brondby going through after winning the Anfield second leg 1-0. In the League Cup Newcastle United won 1-0 at Anfield in round four, Steve Watson on target although the Reds would get their revenge in the Premiership later in the season.

OFF-FIELD

British record £8.5m signing Stan Collymore marked his debut with the winning goal on the opening day of the season against Sheffield Wednesday.

FA Cup top

AWAY MIX

Liverpool mixed and matched during the campaign.

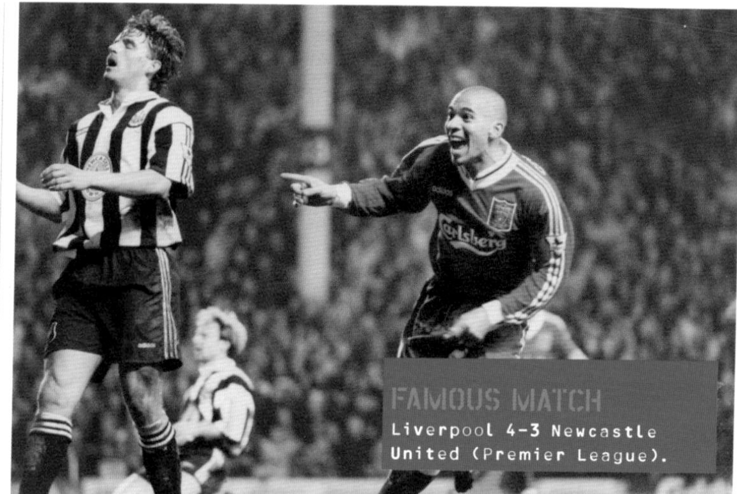

FAMOUS MATCH

Liverpool 4-3 Newcastle United (Premier League).

CUP LOGO

An understated message included on the '96 shirt.

MICKEY T

The back of Michael Thomas's 1996 Cup final jersey.

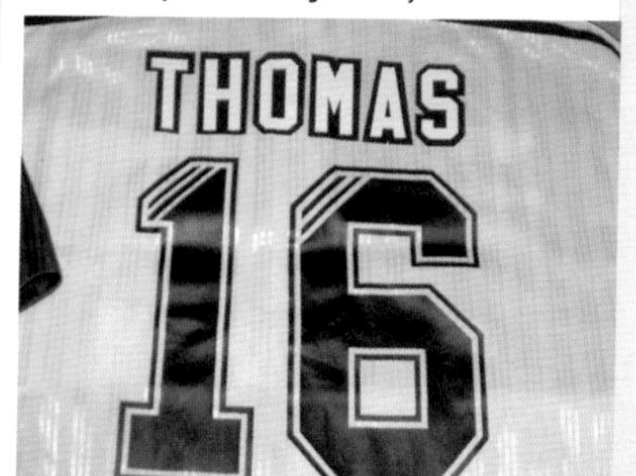

DID YOU KNOW?

Although the 1996 FA Cup final will always be linked with the white Armani suits sported by the Liverpool players before the match, it was also substitute Ian Rush's last game for the club.

Programmes from this historic occasion should be worth a maximum of £40, with tickets around £10.

MANY COLOURS

Liverpool's goalkeeping jerseys could at best be described as `experimental', with both identical in design with the `zig-zag' flash a feature. The bottom shirt was worn by David James in the FA Cup final.

Prem badge

FA CUP RECORD

Ian Rush celebrates with Robbie Fowler (above) after the former had set a new goalscoring record in the FA Cup. Rush's goal against Rochdale, minutes after coming on as a substitute, took his tally in the competition to 42 - one more than Denis Law.

IS LOVE
Reebok

1996-1997

The future's bright, the future's ecru

1996-1997

KIT DESIGN Reebok /// **KIT SPONSOR** Carlsberg

96-97 PLAYERS Jamie Redknapp, Jason McAteer

MANAGER Roy Evans

Reebok 

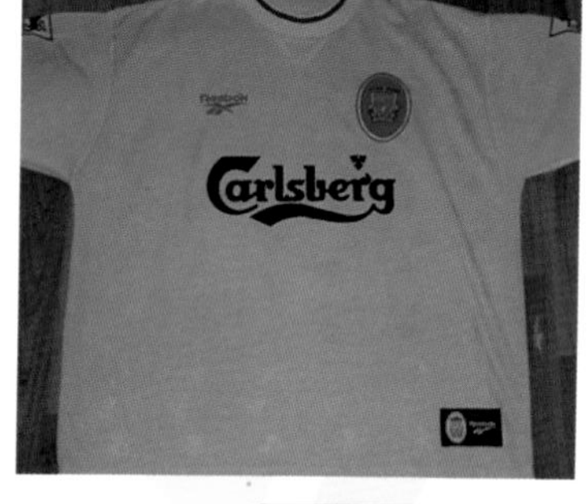

Ecru shirt

ABOUT THE KIT

With a new kit designer came two new Liverpool strips – which included a new away strip that introduced the colour 'ecru' to the football community.

The make-up of the home shirt design changed to include a white stand collar and cuffs, with a Liver bird print incorporated into the shirt material. The 1960s-style oval badge was also reintroduced on both the home and away kits, while the socks had a white Liver bird and Reebok logo woven into the fabric.

The away shirt was officially ecru and graphite (cream and black). Incorporating a crew neck with a small V-neck shape below it, the cream shirt included a Liver bird print, red trim (including the Reebok logo and Liverpool badge) while the kit sponsor logo was in black. The shorts were black with red trim and white logos, or occasionally cream with red trim and logos, while the socks were cream with red Liver birds and black Reebok logos woven in, with red and black bands around the tops.

Home kit

ON-FIELD

Liverpool came closest to European success for the first time in 13 years courtesy of the European Cup Winners' Cup. Drawn against Paris St Germain in the semi-finals, the Reds were 3-0 down from the first leg in France but rallied to pull back two goals in the return...although it proved a goal too far.
In the Premiership Liverpool, Newcastle United and Arsenal all finished on 68 points, but it was the Reds and the Gunners who missed out on the runners-up spot due to goal difference, Roy Evans' side ending the season in fourth.
But there was to be heartbreak in both domestic cup competitions - Middlesbrough claimed a 2-1 home victory in the League Cup quarter-final (a game that saw Jamie Carragher make his first-team bow) while in the FA Cup, a 2-0 half-time lead was squandered as Chelsea won the fourth-round tie 4-2 at Stamford Bridge.

Ecru shirt

OFF-FIELD

Then Liverpool record signing Stan Collymore lasted only two years under Roy Evans before joining his boyhood favourites Aston Villa for £7.5m.

Right: Home top (badge only)

1996-1997

FAMOUS MATCH
Liverpool 4-3 Newcastle United (Premier League).

GOD'S JOB'S A GOOD 'UN

Robbie Fowler created a new Liverpool record following his four-goal haul in the 5-1 victory over Middlesbrough in December 1996 (Fowler celebrates one of the strikes, left). His second of the match saw him beat Ian Rush's previous best by one game in being the quickest to 100, reaching the century in only 165 appearances.

GOD IS NO. 9

It was Robbie Fowler's first season as No. 9 following Ian Rush's departure to Leeds.

CHANGE STRIP

The back of Neil Ruddock's new-look away shirt.

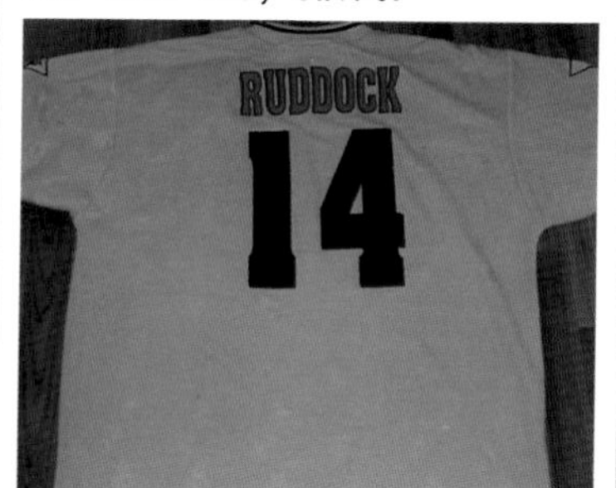

DID YOU KNOW?

Michael Owen became the youngest-ever goalscorer, on his Liverpool debut, when he scored in the 2-1 defeat at Wimbledon in May, 1997. He was 17 years and 144 days old.

A warm local welcome

NO SPONSOR HERE

As occurred the following season, Liverpool's European adventures to France (and also Switzerland in this campaign) saw the ban on alcohol advertising in that country force the club to have their usual sponsor removed from the shirt.

Left: Euro shirt, 96-97

MORE CHOICE

As well as sporting a traditional green goalkeeper's jersey during the season, an 'away' alternative was also sported by David James - an all orange affair which included black Liver bird patterns.

OWEN
18

1997-1998

Out with the old, in with the new

1997-1998

KIT DESIGN Reebok /// **KIT SPONSOR** Carlsberg

97-98 PLAYERS Paul Ince, Oyvind Leonhardsen

MANAGER Roy Evans

Reebok

ABOUT THE KIT

The 'ecru' away strip lasted only one season before being replaced by a predominantly yellow and black version. The shirt was a yellow perforated material with red and black trim on the V-neck and cuffs, with the oval badge included on the shirt and shorts. The shorts were yellow with red stripes down the sides, while the socks were yellow with red tops with the red Liver bird and Reebok logo woven in. Alternative away shorts in dark blue, with a red stripe and yellow band down each side where made around this time, although there is no record that these were ever used. This season also saw the introduction of uniform typeface by the Premier League for the back of shirts.

Home kit

ON-FIELD

The Reds improved on their Premiership showing of the previous campaign to finish in 3rd place behind Double-winners Arsenal and Manchester United – despite Roy Evans' men yielding less points. The nearest we got to claiming any silverware was in the League Cup, when two goals in the opening four minutes saw First Division Middlesbrough claim a 2-0 win in the semi-final, second leg at the Riverside Stadium to win through 3-2 on aggregate. A shock 3-1 home defeat to Coventry City ended FA Cup participation at the third-round stage, while in the UEFA Cup a French team knocked the Reds out of Europe for a second successive season, Strasbourg holding on to claim a 3-2 aggregate triumph.

No logo

OFF-FIELD

John Barnes was allowed to leave on a free transfer in August 1997 after just over 10 years with the club, joining former boss Kenny Dalglish at Newcastle United. Strict French laws on alcohol advertising meant that the famous red strip was short of a sponsorship logo for the UEFA Cup second round, first-leg tie against Strasbourg in France. It is a problem that Carlsberg have got around on occasions since, including using the phrase 'probably', which is synonymous with the company's advertising.

FAMOUS MATCH

Celtic 2-2 Liverpool (UEFA Cup).

PREMIER PATCH

League logo as worn on the red shirt during the season.

BIG BADGE

With inspiration taken from the 1960s, the badge worn on the home shirt between 96-98.

DID YOU KNOW?

An 18-year-old Michael Owen scored 18 Premiership goals, scooping the PFA Young Player of the Year award. As a result he won England senior honours, becoming the youngest England player of the 20th century in the process. He would make his mark on the world stage at the World Cup in France during the summer of 1998.

CHANGE STRIPS

As well as a change to the Liverpool away strip of mainly all yellow, the goalkeeping position also provided some interesting contrasts. The mainly grey and black affair incorporated a sunshine-style flash on both shirt and shorts, and was worn mainly at Anfield. There was also a more sober affair worn away from home, although it was a predominantly lime green hue.

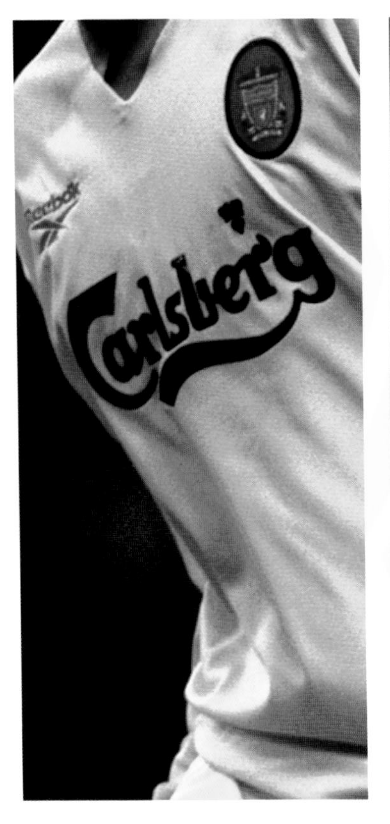

Away shirt

Keeper shirts

1998-1999

Evans, Houllier and old boy returns

1998-1999

KIT DESIGN Reebok /// **KIT SPONSOR** Carlsberg

98-99 PLAYERS Vegard Heggem, Oyvind Leonhardsen

MANAGERS Roy Evans/Gerard Houllier, Gerard Houllier

ABOUT THE KIT

Reebok looked to the 1960s in their inspiration for the new Liverpool home and away strip. The home shirt was made up of a perforated material with white crew neck and cuffs, with the oval badge prominent on shirt and shorts. Like in the 1960s, the shorts included a stripe down the sides (this time in white, rather than red). The socks were red with a white band around the tops.

A V-neck design was introduced to the white away shirt, which was mainly a plain affair with red and black trim, and a red stripe across the shoulders and sleeves.

The shorts were white or black with red stripes down the sides, while the socks were all white with a red and black stripe around the tops.

Home kit

ON-FIELD

It was a sign of the inconsistent form shown in the Premiership that the Reds only managed to secure a seventh-place finish on the final day of the season, courtesy of a 3-0 victory over Wimbledon (narrowly avoiding their worst finish for 37 years in the process). This game also marked the final senior appearance of Steve McManaman in a red shirt ahead of his departure to Real Madrid.
Defeat to Tottenham Hotspur in the League Cup fourth round led to the departure of Roy Evans after a near five-year tenure, a total of 30 years service at Anfield.
There was to be no glory in the FA Cup either, as two late goals saw the Reds suffer an agonising round four exit at Manchester United, while Celta Vigo proved too strong in the UEFA Cup, the Spanish outfit going through 4-1 on aggregate in the third round.

Away 97-99

OFF-FIELD

Phil Thompson was asked to re-join the Anfield coaching staff following Roy Evans' departure in November.

JOINT MANAGERS

Gerard Houllier joined Roy Evans in the summer of 1998, and three wins and a draw in the first four games hinted at possible success. But it didn't take long for results to turn and the partnership to suffer. Evans would depart in November, the pair having resided over only 18 games.

FAMOUS MATCH

Newcastle 1-4 Liverpool (Premier League).

YELLOW SHORTS

Change shorts worn with the yellow away strip.

FIRST NUMBER

Steven Gerrard's first number after coming through the ranks at Liverpool.

DID YOU KNOW?

The win at Newcastle in August (above) was Ruud Gullit's first game in charge of the Magpies.

The 1-1 draw with Chelsea in October saw Phil Babb forced off injured after his attempt to block Pierluigi Casiraghi's goal saw the defender suffer an eye-watering collision with a goal post.

Sub Steven Gerrard made his debut against Blackburn.

August 1998 kit launch

MAN IN BLACK

All black goalkeeper's kits were the norm during the campaign, with the shirt design below of black and grey appearing to resemble the goal netting. The other alternative, as sported by Brad Friedel (left) at a kit launch for the new away strip, introduced different shades of yellow and orange to an all black kit – including 'flame-style' shorts.

1999-2000

Transition as Reds look to the future

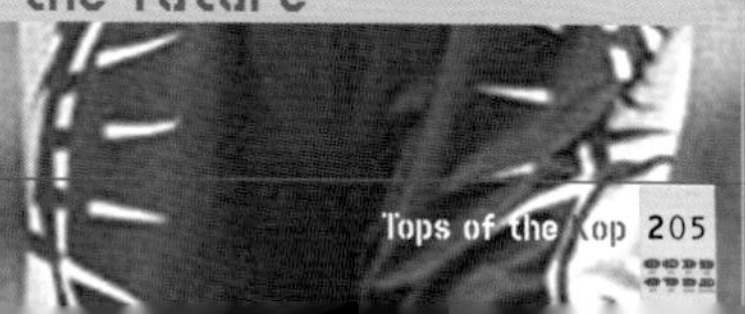

1999-2000

KIT DESIGN Reebok /// **KIT SPONSOR** Carlsberg

99-00 PLAYERS Titi Camara, Stephane Henchoz
MANAGER Gerard Houllier

ABOUT THE KIT

Although the white away kit of the previous season was still used, a new green strip was introduced. The shirt was green with a dark blue and white stand collar. The main body of the shirt also included two white and dark blue diagonal stripes, with the Reebok logo and badge in a central position above the kit sponsor. The shorts were dark blue or green, with green socks incorporating blue tops, or white with blue tops.
The all red home strip also remained unchanged for the season.

Away shirt 1999-2001

ON-FIELD

A season of transition, with manager Gerard Houllier, in sole charge of his first full season building towards the future - a policy that would reap huge rewards the following season.

In the Premiership a poor end to the season meant that the Reds were edged out of a Champions League qualifying spot by Leeds United, finishing fourth and thus having to settle with a UEFA Cup berth. Victory at Bradford City on the final day would have secured third spot, but a 1-0 defeat meant that the only Kopite celebrating was the Bantams' boss Paul Jewell - whose side escaped relegation in the process.

There was little cheer in the domestic cup competitions too, with Blackburn Rovers winning 1-0 at Anfield in the FA Cup fourth round, and Southampton knocking Houllier's men out of the League Cup in round three.

No sponsor

OFF-FIELD

The 1999-2000 season was only the club's third without any involvement in European competition since their first campaign in 1964-65 (excluding the seasons lost due to English clubs' and Liverpoool's absence from overseas competition).

Titi prays

1999-2000

FAMOUS MATCH
Liverpool **3-1** Leeds **United** (Premier League).

CHANGE SHORTS

Worn as an alternative to the usual black away shorts, these are a 'reject' pair as can be recognised by the upside-down Liverpool badge.

PREMIER NUMBER

Design used on Liverpool's Premiership shirts.

DID YOU KNOW?

Six Liverpool players made their debuts in the Premiership opener at Sheffield Wednesday, a 2-1 success.
The Reds failed to find the target in their last five games of the season.

Away shirt, 1998-2000

THUNDERBIRD

This goalkeeping affair complemented the green away strip, bringing to mind the 'Thunderbirds-style' design of Crystal Palace's strip from the late 70s and early 80s.

2000-2001

Treble champions

2000-2001

KIT DESIGN Reebok /// **KIT SPONSOR** Carlsberg

00-01 PLAYERS Michael Owen, Gary McAllister

MANAGER Gerard Houllier

Reebok 

Kit launch 2000

Premier League logo

ABOUT THE KIT

New home and away kits were launched – proving to be something of a success come the conclusion of the season. The all-red home strip included white piping down the sleeves and the return of a red V-neck stand collar, with white trim. The shorts had white piping around the legs while a white Liver bird (middle) and Reebok logo (top) was woven into the socks.

The new away kit was gold with dark blue sides and a blue V-neck stand collar. The shorts were blue with gold stripes down the sides, with change shorts of gold and blue stripes. The socks were blue with gold tops, while the logos were the same as for the home socks. On this kit, Michael Owen was quoted in 2002 as claiming the kit was his favourite Liverpool strip. "My favourite is the gold one because of the FA Cup final. Someone can show me it in 50 years time and I'll think: `That's the one we won the FA Cup in'."

Interestingly Reebok used their type-face logo for the shirt, but sportswear logo (and no type-face)for the shorts. Incidentally, the green and dark blue away kit from the previous season was still in use, mainly as a third kit.

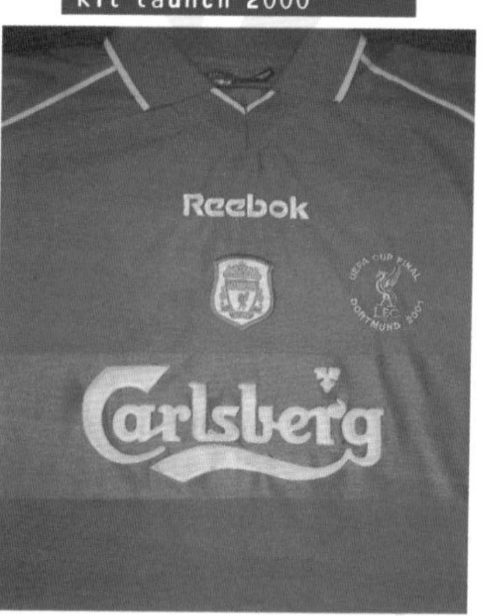

UEFA Cup final shirt

ON-FIELD

A season difficult to be beaten for drama, excitement and success, 2000-2001 signalled a dramatic return to trophy-winning form after a near six-year drought.

The first of the three successes, the League Cup, was secured courtesy of a penalty shoot-out, the Reds having conceded a last-minute penalty against Birmingham City (the match finished 1-1 after extra time).

Two late goals from Michael Owen stunned Arsenal in the FA Cup final, and four days later the UEFA Cup was secured in equally dramatic fashion, the Reds twice losing a two-goal advantage against Spanish side Alaves before winning courtesy of a golden goal own goal in extra time by defender Delfi Geli to provail 5-4.

In a marathon end to the campaign, Liverpool still needed to play their last league match three days later, with a victory confirming a Champions League qualifying spot - and this they duly did in style, Charlton Athletic being swept aside 4-0 at The Valley.

FA Cup final shirt, and logo (below)

OFF-FIELD

A total of 11 players made their first-team debuts for the Reds during the season, including Nick Barmby (£6m), Christian Ziege (£5.5m) and Igor Biscan (£5.5m).

It was the first season that the club have reached the Champions League qualifiers.

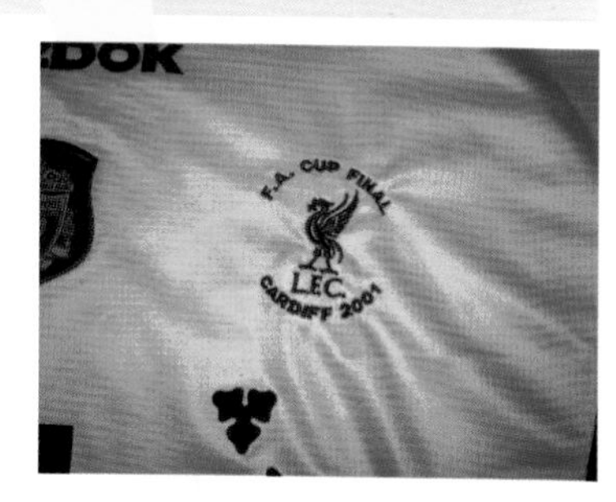

FAMOUS MATCH

Liverpool 5-4 Alaves (aet) (UEFA Cup final).

FA CUP SPONSORED BY...

Official sponsor's logo, which was first worn on the shirt sleeves of the finalists when sponsored by Littlewoods for the 1996 clash between the Reds and Manchester United.

FINAL LIVER BIRDS

The logos (below) were displayed in each of Liverpool's successful Cup finals wearing red shirts - the yellow away kit being worn in the FA Cup final.

DID YOU KNOW?

The treble achieved was the first time any English team had won three cup competitions in one season. Liverpool were the first team to win a major final via the Golden Goal rule (UEFA). Estimated programme and ticket stub values:
League Cup - £20 for both;
FA Cup - Programme £6, ticket £10;
UEFA Cup - Programme £7, ticket £15.

GLORY IN YELLOW

Michael Owen's favourite shirt was the first time the club had won the FA Cup in a different kit than the traditional all red. Indeed, in terms of domestic finals, the Reds have only won the League Cup once (1981) wearing their away strip.

SANDER, NO. 1

Liverpool's Dutch stopper has his shirt displayed in the Liverpool club museum from this historic campaign.

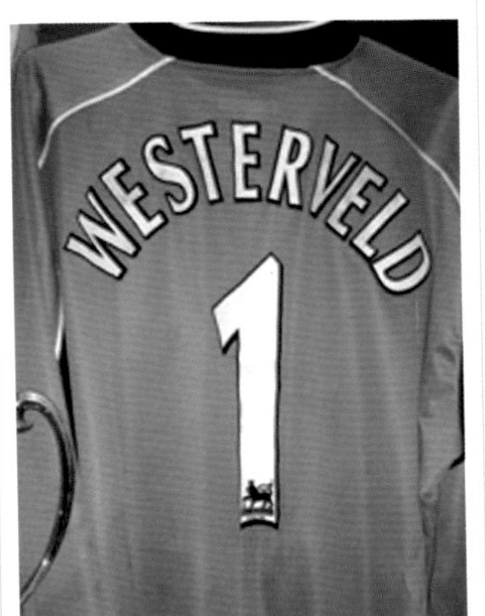

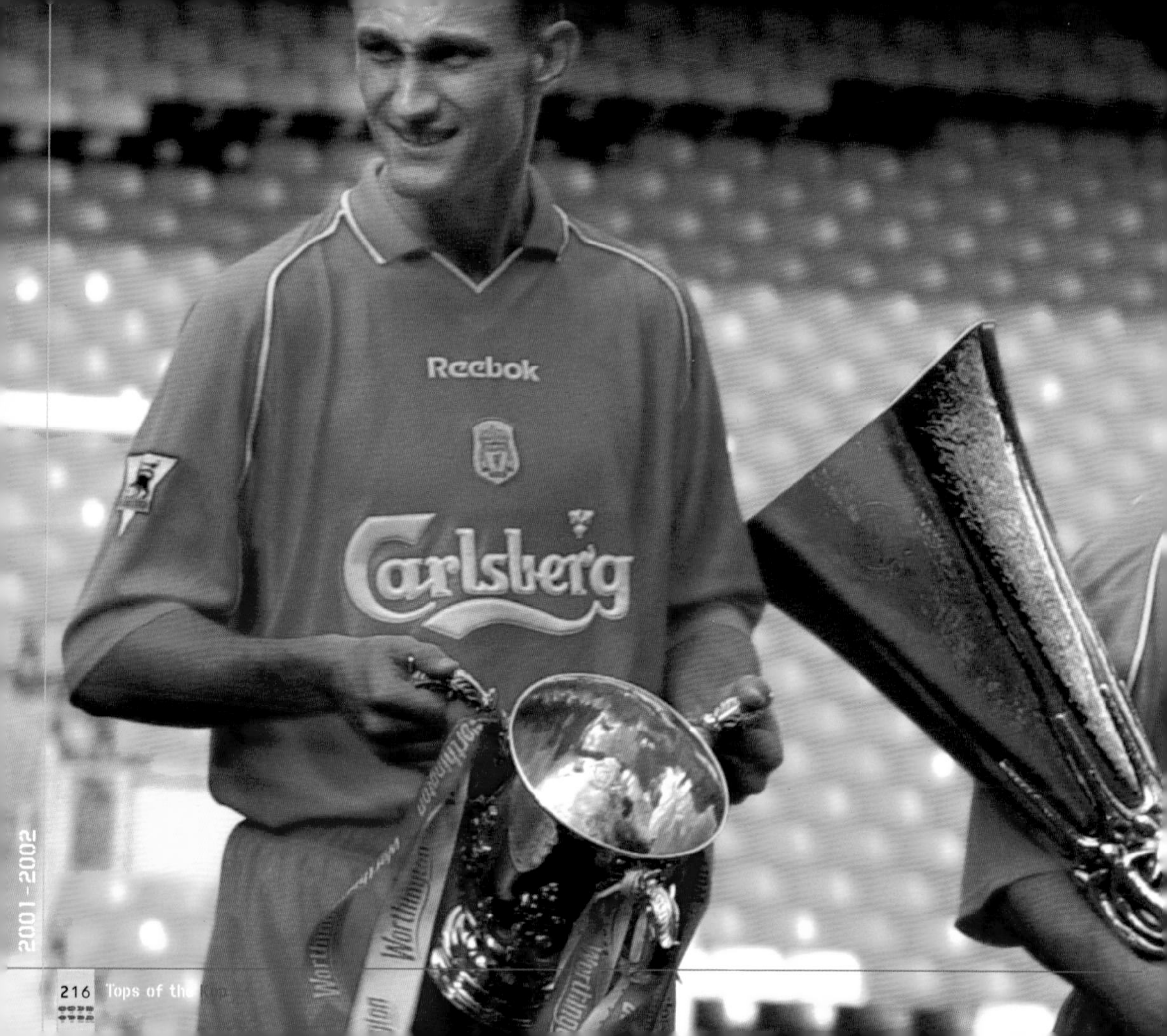
Reebok
Carlsberg
Worthington

2001-2002

Five titles, runners-up and Euro woe

2001-2002

KIT DESIGN Reebok /// **KIT SPONSOR** Carlsberg

01-02 PLAYERS Jari Litmanen, Danny Murphy
MANAGER Gerard Houllier

ABOUT THE KIT

Although the home strip remained unchanged, a different version was introduced to commemorate the club's debut season in the Champions League. Designed to resemble the classic Liverpool kits of the 1970s, the shirt incorporated a white V-neck and cuffs, with the sponsor logos in yellow, rather than the usual white. The usual badge design was also altered, with four stars now added above the badge to represent the number of European Cup wins. This was also moved to the centre of the shirt.
The new away kit was white with a V-neck blue trim and yellow piping, which included a new shield on the top and short and a more modern Reebok type-face. Two different shorts were also released – white with blue and yellow trim, or blue with yellow and white trim. Similarly the socks were either white with blue tops and a yellow band, or blue with white tops and a yellow band. The kit had actually been previwed the previous season in the UEFA Cup semi-final first leg against Barcelona at the Nou Camp.

Euro kit

ON-FIELD

A Premiership runners-up spot behind Arsenal was solid reward for a Liverpool team who built on the cup successes of the previous season. Indeed, the FA Charity Shield and European Super Cup were secured in August, meaning the club held five different titles at the same time for the remainder of 2001.
In the club's debut season in the Champions League, Houllier led the Reds to the quarter-finals, before suffering an agonising defeat to eventual runners-up Bayer Leverkusen. In the domestic cup competitions, there were early exits in the FA Cup (round four) and League Cup (round three).

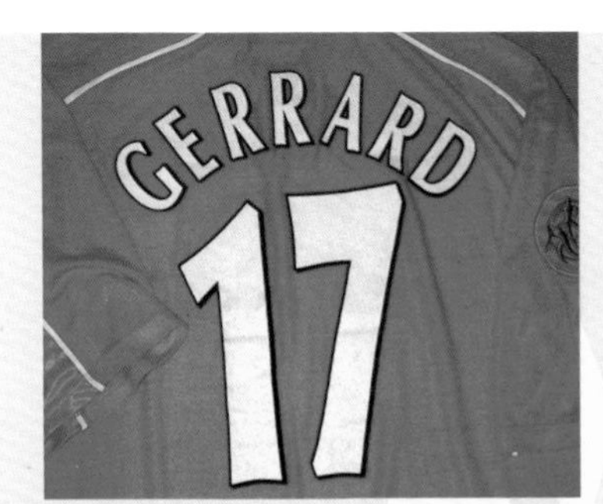

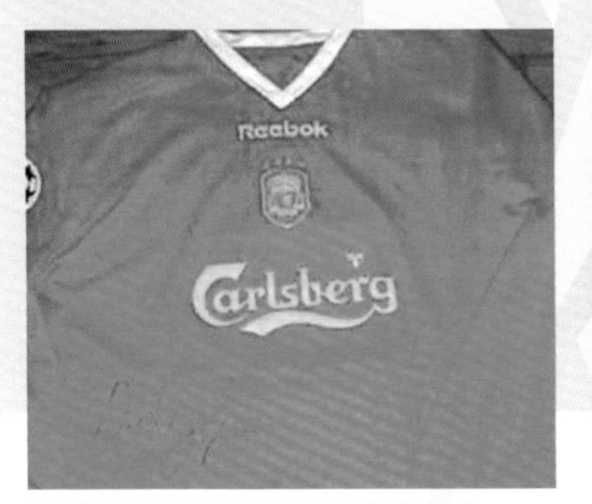

OFF-FIELD

Gerard Houllier was taken ill during half-time against Leeds United in October 2001 - emergency heart surgery followed. His assistant Phil Thompson took charge as a result while he recovered, finally taking his place on the bench on an emotional occasion against AS Roma in the Champions League the following March.
Robbie Fowler joined Leeds United in mid-season for a club-record sale £11m.

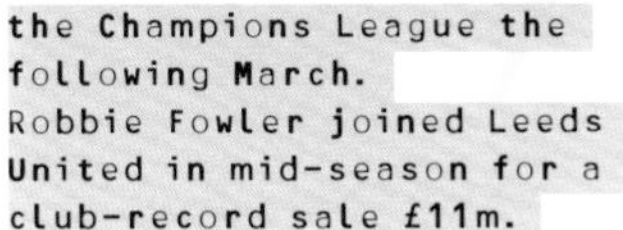

Home kits

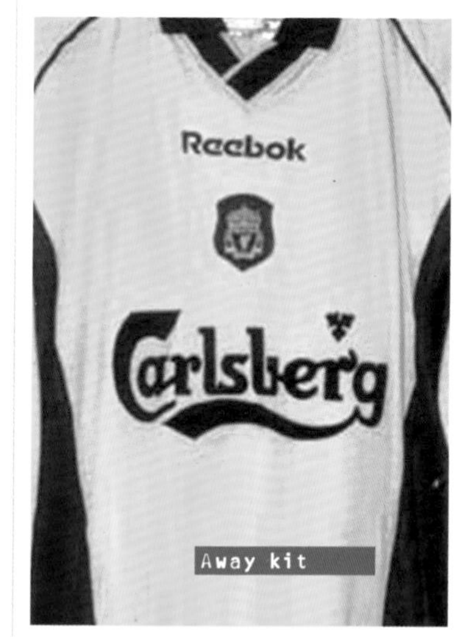

Away kit

FAMOUS MATCH

Liverpool 2-0 AS Roma (Champions League).

SUPER CUP

Sleeve logos used for the 2001 showpiece against Bayern Munich in Monaco.

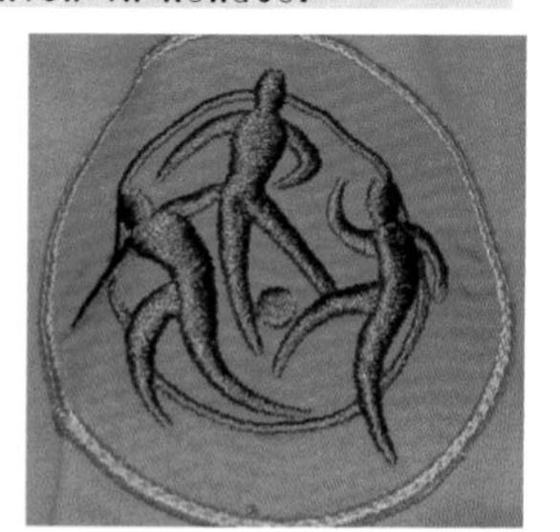

FOUR STARS

Badge used on the European strip of 2001-2003.

DID YOU KNOW?

The FA Charity Shield and European Super Cup wins in August 2001 meant that Liverpool were the first team to win five trophies in six months.

Estimated programme and ticket stub valuations:

FA Charity Shield – Programme £10+, ticket £5; European Super Cup – Ticket £15, programme £5.

Away kit

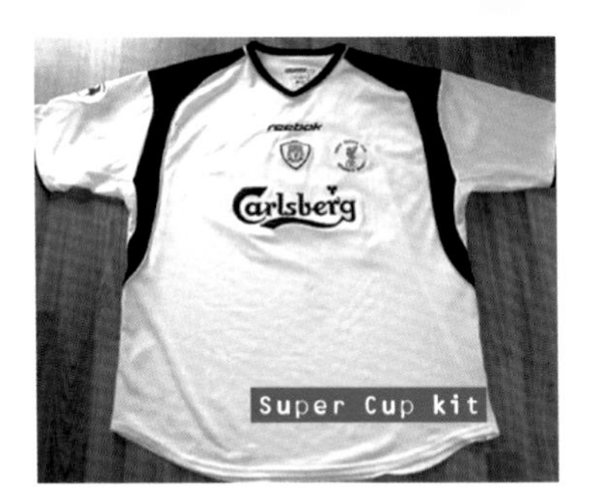

Super Cup kit

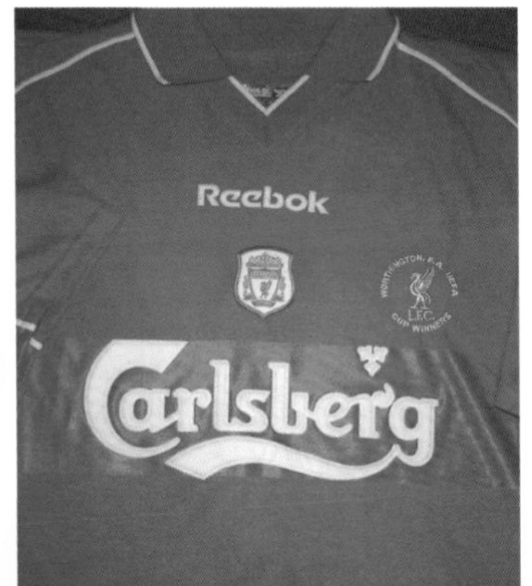

SPECIAL EDITION

There was a special edition shirt released to commemorate the historic 2000-2001 season. In a similar vein to the yellow `special' released ahead of the 1986-1987 season following the Double-winning campaign, this version incorporated an extra Liver bird logo. The FA Cup, League Cup and UEFA Cup triumphs were signified although to our knowledge, the shirt was never worn in a first-team match.

FIRST DERBY

There were celebrations all round for Jerzy Dudek, as his first derby match ended with a 3-1 win at Goodison Park. As well as the green and black affair of the previous season, this goalkeeping kit was deemed an alternative choice, with the yellow jersey complete with black sleeves and black/grey pattern design, black shorts and socks with yellow trim.

2002-2003

Euro adventures...and Cardiff joy (again)

2002-2003

KIT DESIGN Reebok /// KIT SPONSOR Carlsberg

02-03 PLAYERS Dietmar Hamann, El-Hadji Diouf
MANAGER Gerard Houllier

Reebok 

Charity Shield '02

ABOUT THE KIT

New home and away kits were designed, styled deliberately to resemble 'armour'. Designed by Reebok's Jo Booth, the process took into account the latest trends in styling, fabrics, colours and logos, with the idea of body armour pursued while also maintaining the traditions of the club.
The home kit was given a more traditional Liverpool hue based on kits from the 70s and 80s, unlike previous Reebok kits. The red on the shirt was striped on the back, while the badge was moved to the centre on both home and away kits. The idea behind the seam pattern being deliberately shaped like body armour was for purposes of comfort and ease of movement, rather than traditionally down the sides (see sketch, bottom right of original design ideas). The shorts were all red with white logos, with the socks incorporating 'LFC' on the tops and logos in the middle.
The away strip changed to black for the first time in the club's history, which also included silver triangles on the sleeves, with a red stripe on the V-neck and cuffs. The shorts were silver with red stripe, or black with a red stripe, while the socks were black with silver and black tops, or black with silver tops and a red trim.
The reason for the change to black was revealed by Booth in an interview with LFC Magazine in 2002: "(It was) a case of doing something a little bit different, a little bit sharper, rather than churning out the same old colour again."

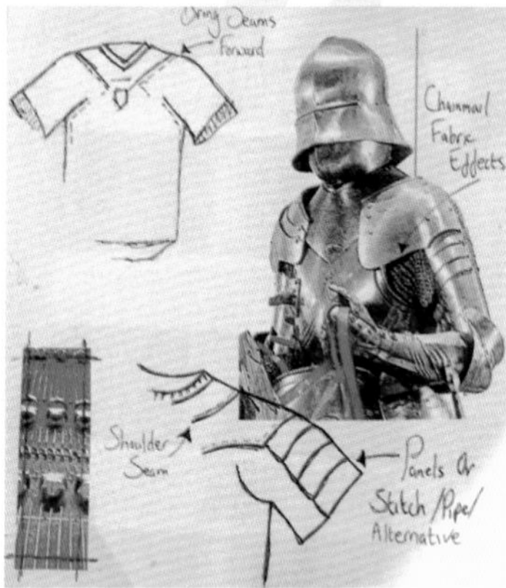

ON-FIELD

Although Liverpool clinched a memorable League Cup triumph for the seventh time, a 2-0 victory over Manchester United at the Millennium Stadium, disappointment in other competitions at home and abroad would ultimately overshadow the campaign. In the Premiership, the Reds lost fourth spot to Chelsea on the final day of the season in a 'winner-takes-all' encounter, going down 2-1 at Stamford Bridge having taken the lead. In the FA Cup there was defeat to Crystal Palace in a fourth-round replay at Anfield (2-0), while the Reds bowed out of the Champions League at the first group stage, finishing third in their group of four. Finishing third meant a UEFA Cup lifeline, although Celtic proved too strong over two legs in the quarter-finals, winning 3-1 on aggregate. For the record, the season's curtain-raiser saw Arsenal win the FA Community Shield clash 2-1.

OFF-FIELD

Amongst the club's transfer dealings in the summer of 2002 were Salif Diao, Bruno Cheyrou and El-Hadji Diouf - the trio costing a combined total of over £18m.

Steven Gerrard (quoted in August 2002):
"It's a better Liverpool red and it's more comfy."

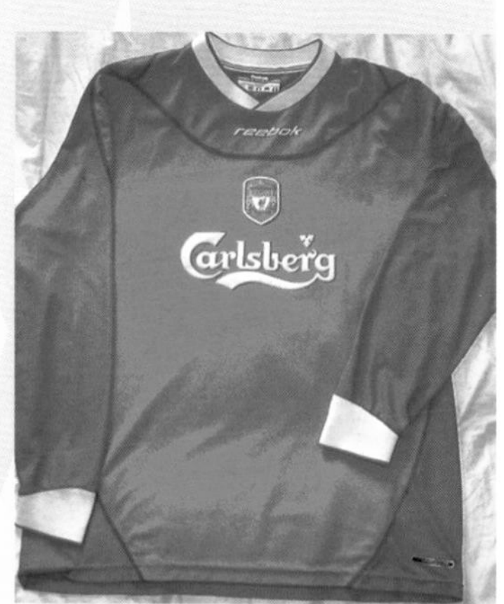

Home shirts worn in 02-03

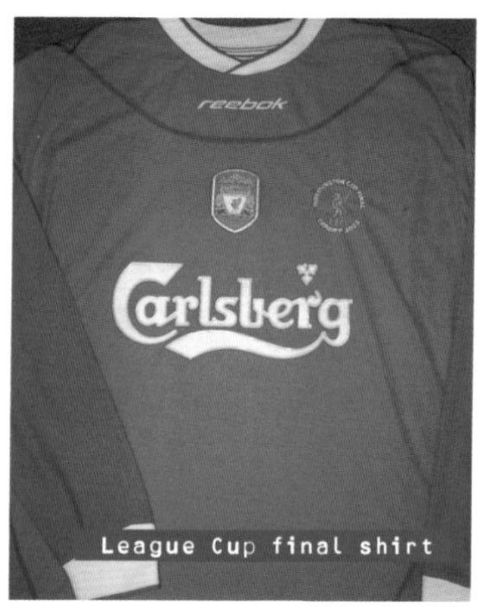

League Cup final shirt

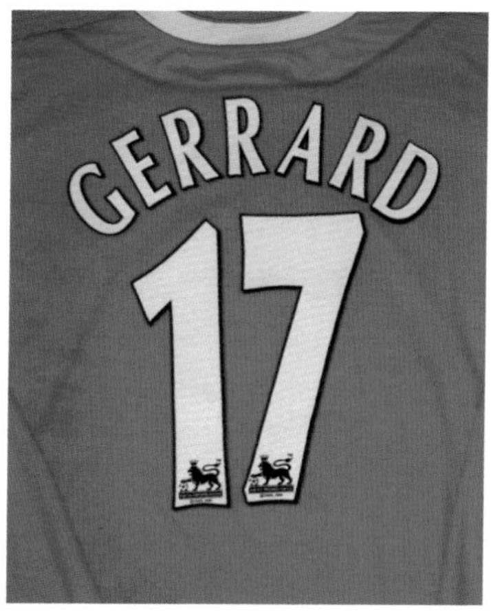

FAMOUS MATCH

Liverpool 2-0 Manchester United (League Cup final).

LEAGUE CUP LOGO

Whilst keeping the usual badge in the centre of the shirt, this simplified logo was added for the League Cup final – incorporating the sponsor's name.

EURO TOUCHES

Introduced on the European strip the previous season, the gold badge reflected the four European Cup wins in the form of four gold stars. The official Champions League logo is taken from the black away strip.

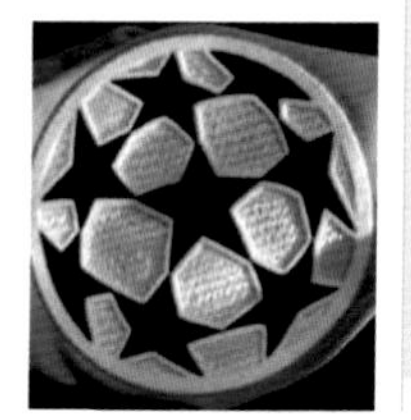

DID YOU KNOW?

The defeat to Arsenal in the FA Community Shield (newly-named that year) was the club's first at the Millennium Stadium. Liverpool's failure to go beyond the first group stage of the Champions League had much to do with a certain Rafael Benitez, whose Valencia side beat the Reds both home and away. Incidentally, the Champions League strip of the previous season was worn again in both European competitions.

Away shirt

The League Cup final success over Manchester United extended Liverpool's record to seven wins in the competition. Two programmes were issued – one with the word `official' while the other was `offical'.
The mis-spelt version is the more common, and only worth around £5 while the correctly spelt is worth nearer the £30 mark.

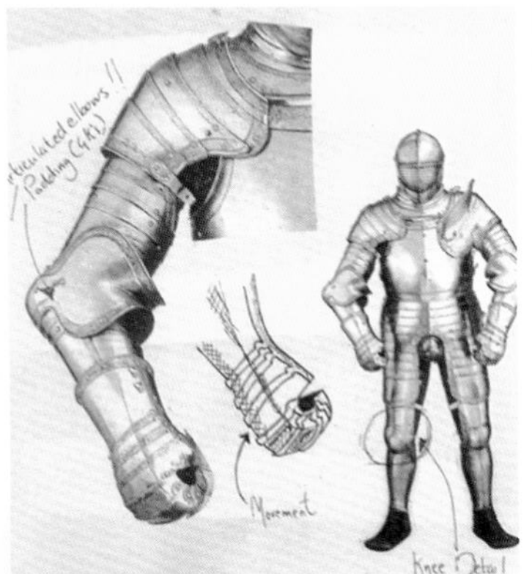

AWAY DESIGNS

Further plans made in the planning process for Liverpool's first black away strip, which began in 2001.

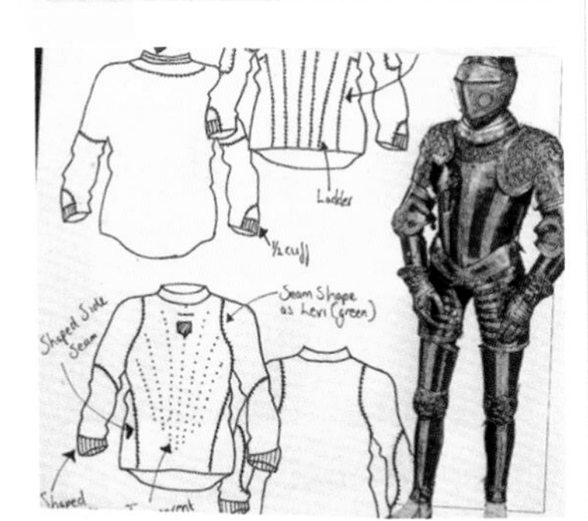

MEN IN BLACK

The home goalkeeper kit was an all black affair with grey and red touches, as worn by Chris Kirkland (below) during the campaign.

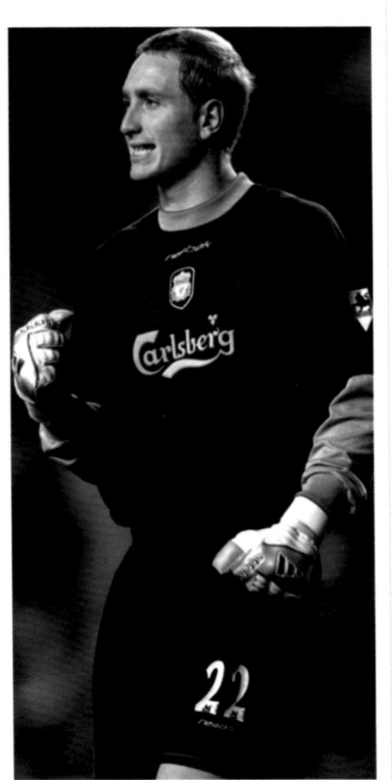

Carlsberg
Carlsberg

2003-2004

Cup blows and the end for Houllier

2003-2004

KIT DESIGN Reebok /// **KIT SPONSOR** Carlsberg

03-04 PLAYERS Harry Kewell, Bruno Cheyrou

MANAGER Gerard Houllier

ABOUT THE KIT

The black and silver away kit experiment lasted one season before a return to more traditional white. A red and black stripe was included down the arms, both sides of the ribs and around the neck. The badge also changed from the shield to an oval shape on the shirt and shorts, with the Reebok typeface being replaced with the Reebok logo (now included within a badge), and the *Carlsberg* logo written in the company colour of green. The shorts were black with red piping, or white with red piping, while the socks were white with a black 'L.F.C.' and a black square with red piping on the tops, or black with grey and red piping on the tops with a 'L.F.C.' legend and Reebok logo.

Away kit

ON-FIELD

Having set out with ambitions to mount an assault on the Premiership title, the Reds' inconsistency meant a fourth-place finish. Although this secured a valuable Champions League qualification spot (as the following season proved), champions Arsenal finished a massive 30 points ahead. There was little joy in the cup competitions too. There were exits at the hands of Portsmouth in the FA Cup fifth round and to eventual runners-up Bolton Wanderers in the League Cup, while Marseille edged out the Reds in the last 16 of the UEFA Cup.

OFF-FIELD

Gerard Houllier left the club at the end of the season with a year still left on his contract. Despite securing Champions League qualification, it was not deemed enough to satisfy the Liverpool board.

No 8

2003-2004

FAMOUS MATCH

Everton 0-3 Liverpool (Premier League).

ASIA TOUR 2003

The usual home strip, retained from 2002-03, was given a logo below the club badge for games on the two-match tour in the pre-season of 2003.

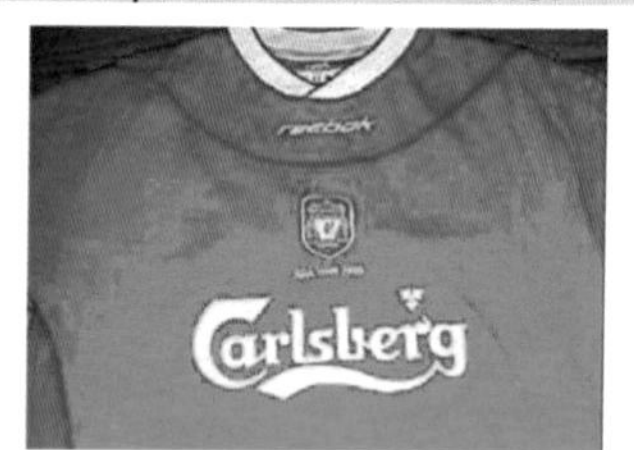

PREMIER NUMBER

El-Hadji Diouf was the first No 9 in Liverpool history to fail to register a single goal during the campaign.

DID YOU KNOW?

The 3-0 victory at Goodison Park was the Reds' biggest against Everton since 1986.
Michael Owen broke Ian Rush's European goalscoring record against Olimpija Ljubljana – his 21st in Europe.
On-loan goalkeeper Paul Jones became the oldest player to make his debut for the club since World War 2, aged 36 years, 8 months and 23 days old.

SHIRT LOGOS

Originally an addition to shirt sleeves during the final days of the First Division at the start of the 1990s, an official League logo has been worn on shirts in the top flight throughout the FA Premier League's existence.

The logo displayed at the bottom of the page is taken from the 2003-04 home shirt, with the official sponsor now added to the name of the English top flight.

The home shirt during this period also displayed a 'Hydromove' logo (right). An official Reebok trademark, the logo highlighted the quality of the fabric, the theory being that it would provide the player with maximum comfort in all seasons.

THREE KEEPERS

Two kits were produced by Reebok for the campaign. Paul Jones (right), who became the club's oldest post-War debutant in his two-game loan spell, wore a slight variation to the launch kit which included black shorts and grey socks. The yellow kit, which was used the previous season, was a similar style with the top yellow with black trim, black shorts and socks. The other release was dark orange and purple, with purple shorts and orange socks.

Shirt logo

Yellow...

...and orange

2003-2004 continued

Carlsberg

2004-2005

Istanbul and all that...

2004-2005

KIT DESIGN Reebok /// **KIT SPONSOR** Carlsberg

04-05 PLAYERS Jamie Carragher, Xabi Alonso

MANAGER Rafael Benitez

ABOUT THE KIT

Two new kits welcomed the Spanish revolution at Anfield ahead of the 2004-05 season. The new home shirt incorporated an octagon-shaped all-red collar, with areas under the arms being the only real white patches on the shirt, apart from logos. The badge surround was also changed from previous kits, while other features included 'Play Dry' material and a diagonal shadow pattern. The shorts and socks were red, apart from the logos.

The away strip was pale yellow and black, with the main shirt sponsors' logo in green print. The main feature of the shirt was the tyre track black pattern on the right (top) side of the chest and left (bottom). The shorts were black with yellow trim, or yellow with black trim – as were the socks.

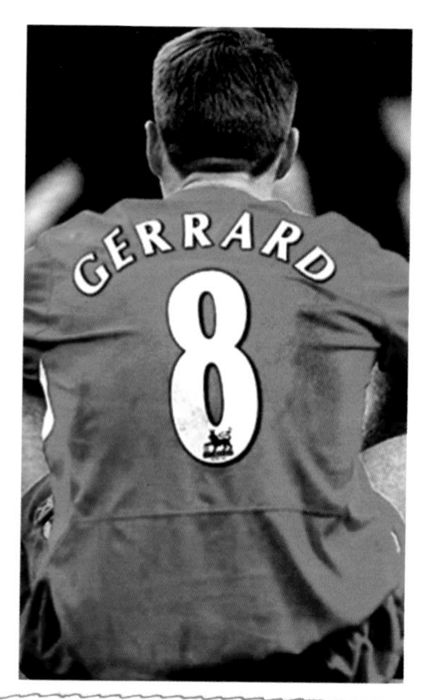

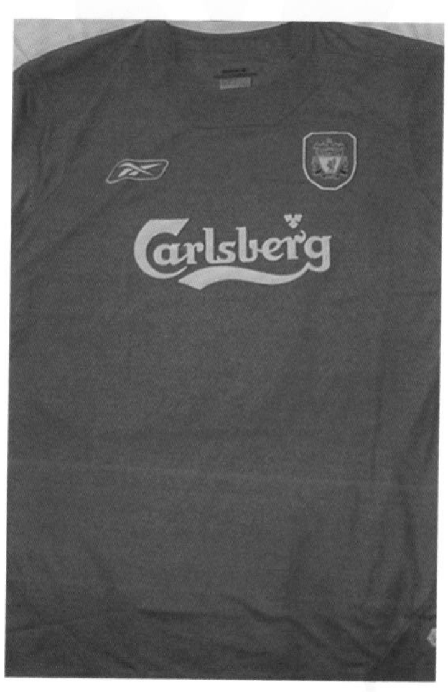

Home kit

ON-FIELD

The stunning, unexpected Champions League final success over AC Milan overshadowed what had been a generally disappointing season in term of league results. Liverpool were kept out of the top four qualifying spots for the following season's competition by neighbours Everton, finishing in fifth place while there had been a shock exit at the hands of Burnley in the FA Cup third round (although the Reds did field a weakened line-up). There was disappointment in the League Cup final, as Jose Mourinho's Chelsea edged a five-goal thriller in Cardiff although it was the big one that more than made up for this disappointment...

OFF-FIELD

Liverpool legend Emlyn Hughes passes away at the age of 57 from a brain tumour.

Away 04-06

'05 Champions League final

FAMOUS MATCH

Liverpool 3-3 AC Milan (aet)
(Champions League final).

USA TOUR SHIRT

A central tour logo was added to the home shirt for Liverpool's summer 2004 tour.

USA TOUR LOGOS

The logos worn on home and away shorts on the USA tour.

DID YOU KNOW?

Liverpool's fifth European Cup triumph made England the most successful country in European competition (with the least number of losses to wins). Incidentally, after Arsenal's European Cup final defeat to Barcelona in 2006, that honour was regained by Spain.
The 3-0 comeback to win against AC Milan was the first such instance in the showpiece final.

03-05 away

DIFFERENT JERZYS

All green was regular sported by Polish stopper Jerzy Dudek during the campaign (below), although as the Istanbul celebrations show, black and purple were the lucky colours for all concerned in Istanbul. In the celebrations, Dudek was quoted as stating: "I am in the heaven."

AND ANOTHER THING

Mrs Montse Benitez, Rafa's wife, had a premonition that Liverpool would win the Champions League a month before the final. It was also revealed that she had experienced similar premonitions in the lead-up to her husband's La Liga and UEFA Cup triumphs when in charge of Valencia.

CUP
THE SWIGGERS
REINA

2005-2006

Gerrard in seventh heaven

2005-2006

KIT DESIGN Reebok /// KIT SPONSOR Carlsberg

05-06 PLAYERS Steven Gerrard, Luis Garcia
MANAGER Rafael Benitez

No sponsor

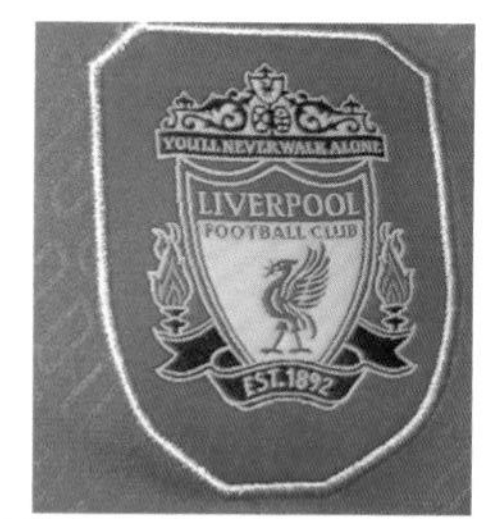

ABOUT THE KIT

The final season under Reebok led to the introduction of two new kits. The first was another limited edition European strip, all red with gold trim which now carried five gold stars – one for each European Cup triumph. A new white away kit was also introduced, the top including red and black trim and a green sponsor's logo, worn with either black or white shorts and socks.

European kit

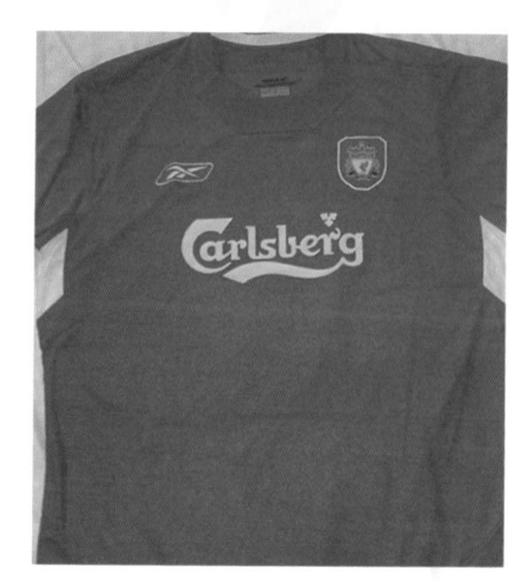

Home kit

ON-FIELD

For a second successive season, Rafael Benitez led the Reds to a dramatic Cup-winning triumph. The penalty shoot-out triumph was Liverpool's ninth in 10, helping secure a seventh FA Cup success thanks to Steven Gerrard's stunning late intervention with West Ham leading 3-2 late on in normal time. In the lead-up to the Cardiff final, Benitez's men had won 11 successive matches, helping secure third in the Premiership.

A weakened line-up put paid to progress in the League Cup (losing 2-1 at Crystal Palace in round three) and despite a 3-0 aggregate defeat to Benfica in the last 16 of the Champions League, a third European Super Cup was secured courtesy of a 3-1 extra-time victory over UEFA Cup holders CSKA Moscow. Liverpol were also involved in the inaugural Club World Championship in December, and were unfortunate to lose the final 1-0 to Sao Paolo.

Yellow away

OFF-FIELD

Liverpool were granted special dispensation to enter the Champions League, despite not finishing in the top four of the Premiership the previous season. Their Champions League success meant that UEFA were lobbied to let the Reds defend their title, who eventually relented, although Liverpool were forced to enter at the first qualifying stage, meaning a mid-July start to their season.

FAMOUS MATCH

Liverpool 3-3 West Ham Utd (aet) (FA Cup final).

CAPITAL OF CULTURE

To celebrate Liverpool's status for 2008, Steven Gerrard and James Beattie were permitted to wear '08' during the March 2006 derby. It proved a mixed day for Gerrard, who was sent off after only 18 minutes – but the Reds still won 3-1!

EURO COLOUR

The gold numbering and letters matched the trim of the European kit (right), with the home Premiership and domestic cup version remaining white (left).

DID YOU KNOW?

In a season of new records, the team went 10 consecutive games without conceding a goal, and set a new Liverpool Premiership record of 82 points.
The Reds had three goals disallowed in the Club World Championship final against Sao Paolo – the first time this has occured in a major final.

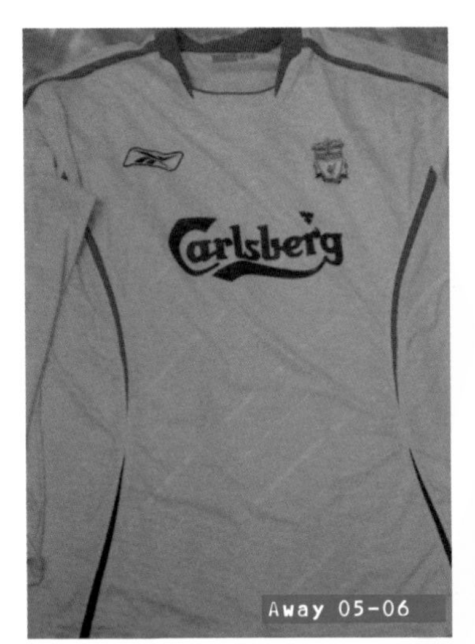

Away 05-06

LOGO ADDITIONS

Extra additions to the shirt worn in the European Super Cup final, with the logo on the left worn on the arms.

Left: Super Cup badge

GOALKEEPING OPTIONS

A home goalkeeping kit of traditional green and black was sported throughout the season by first choice Jose Reina, while the all yellow with black and white trim was worn primarily for away games.

2005–2006 continued

PIRELLI
19
Carlsb
ay

2006-2008

Three stripes on our shirt

2006-2008

KIT DESIGN adidas /// KIT SPONSOR Carlsberg

06-08 **PLAYERS** Fernando Torres, Javier Mascherano
MANAGER Rafael Benitez

ABOUT THE KIT

The return to adidas saw the classic 'three stripes' back. Three new kits - red home, and two change strips of yellow and white and green were launched for 2006-07. There was a return of the collar and white piping, with the unique three stripes also featuring prominently. The shield was removed from behind the Liver bird crest, and a Liver bird was embossed on the back.
The yellow kit was similar, the white touches of the home shirt instead being in red.
The white strip, used mainly as an away European kit, had green down the left arm and side, continuing down onto the shorts. The right side of the top and shorts was white and the socks white with green tops and white stripes. The logos remained green on both away kits, while on all shorts, unusually the adidas logo is positioned on the back left (a feature maintained for 07-08). 'FlowMapping', 'ClimaCool' and 'ForMotion' reflected advanced shirt design technology on the shirts (the latter two again being an 07-08 feature), while the left sleeve of each shirt included the adidas football symbol (bottom right), used by the company since early 2006.
The 2007-08 campaign saw two new away kits launched. The main change strip (inspired by the 1970s away kit) was a white shirt, black shorts and white socks, with red trim including the unique three stripes; any semblance of green is used on the badge and shirt sponsor.
The third strip, dubbed as the European away kit, was mainly all black, with white trim and a red graphic surrounding the central area of the shirt. This is also prominent in the corner of the shorts.

Euro shirt

Home shirt

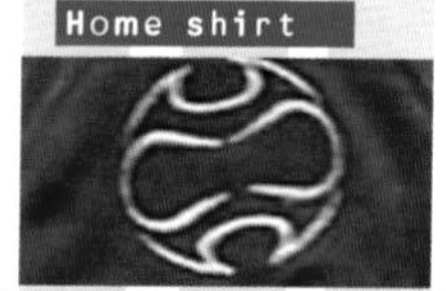

adidas football symbol

ON-FIELD

League underachivement was tempered by the club's continued prosperity in the Champions League.
A second final in three years, again against AC Milan (this time in Athens) ended in a 2-1 defeat in 2007, while 2007-08 saw the Reds recover from a poor early group campaign to challenge again in the knockout phase, a sixth crown remaining in sight following defeat of Inter Milan in the last 16.
A Premier League title challenge rarely threatened during the period, despite third place being achieved in 06-07 and another high finish certain in 2008.
An FA Community Shield was achieved in August 2006 courtesy of a 2-1 defeat of Chelsea, but largely the domestic cup competitions have proved fruitless, with Arsenal inflicting defeats in th FA Cup third round and in the last eight of the League Cup in 06-07, while Barnsley (round five) and Chelsea (last eight) did likewise in the FA Cup and League Cup respectively in 07-08.

07-08 3rd kit

OFF-FIELD

February 2007 saw the historic takeover of the club by American tycoons George Gillett and Tom Hicks, with plans for a new stadium situated next to Anfield on Stanley Park unveiled.
Fernando Torres became the club's record signing when joining in the summer of 2007 from Atletico Madrid.
The Spanish international would make a huge impact in his first season at Anfield, becoming the first Reds player to score 20 league goals since Robbie Fowler.

06-07 Away shirt

06-07 3rd kit number

adidas kit launch 2006

FAMOUS MATCH

Liverpool 1-0 Chelsea (aet) (Champions League).

NO SPONSOR

Shirt worn without sponsor in Bordeaux, Toulouse and Marseille due to French laws regarding alcohol advertising.

NUMBERS GAME

Craig Bellamy's Premiership number (left), and a more European appearance (right).

DID YOU KNOW?

Xabi Alonso's 65-yard wonder strike against Newcastle United in September 2006 was recorded as the furthest out any Liverpool player has scored in a first-team game.
The win over Aston Villa in August 2007 saw the club surpass 1000 Premier League points.
The 8-0 defeat of Besiktas in 07-08 was a Champions League record.

06-07 3rd kit

07-08 Away kit

GOALKEEPER KIT

Jose Reina sports the 2006-08 home keeper strip (below), while the mainly black kit (centre page, bottom) was the away strip in 06-07. A change strip of all green was worn in 07-08 (bottom).

MISCELLANEOUS

Training kits, manager garb and kit ads

THE MANAGERS

King Kenny, Gerard's scarf and Roy Evans

KENNY

The famous images (left) of the original 'King Kenny' coat from the late 1980s and early 1990s. Provided by Liverpool FC museum curator Stephen Done, the coat was donated by the man himself and is one of a few coats he had in supply during the period.

GERARD & ROY

On display in the club museum, Gerard Houllier's original scarf was a regular touchline feature during the latter part of his stint in charge, including his famous return against AS Roma in 2002.
The picture of Roy Evans meanwhile is taken in the wake of the 1995 League Cup success.

MISCELLANEOUS

PVC, fizzy pop, Tsunami Soccer Aid and 90s garb

PVC EFFORT

Liverpool fan Howard Gray, a member of kings of 1990s dance music Apollo 440 was provided with one of the most unusual LFC kit replicas. An engineer on the 'Anfield Rap' in 1988 and who helped put together the 1996 Cup final song, his then girlfriend got a tighter than normal replica of the classic 1980s kit reproduced for a fancy dress party.

SOCCER AID

The original Liverpool Legends shirt as worn for the Tsunami Soccer Aid charity match at Anfield on Easter Monday 2005. Over 39,000 saw the match, a 6-2 victory for the Reds over a Celebrity XI team, with the event helping to raise over £500,000.

Centenary T-shirt

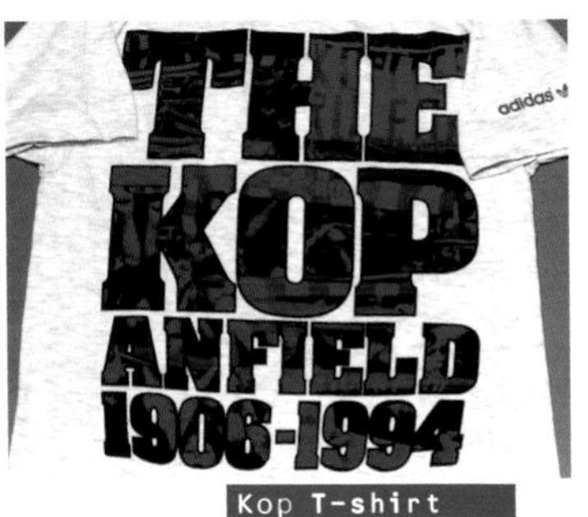

Kop T-shirt

TRAINING TOPS

1977, Sammy Lee, 90s selections and Istanbul

1977 European Cup final

Sammy Lee waterproof

ISTANBUL

Original players' tracksuit top as worn on the night of the historic Champions League final triumph in Turkey, May 2005.

Late 1990s version

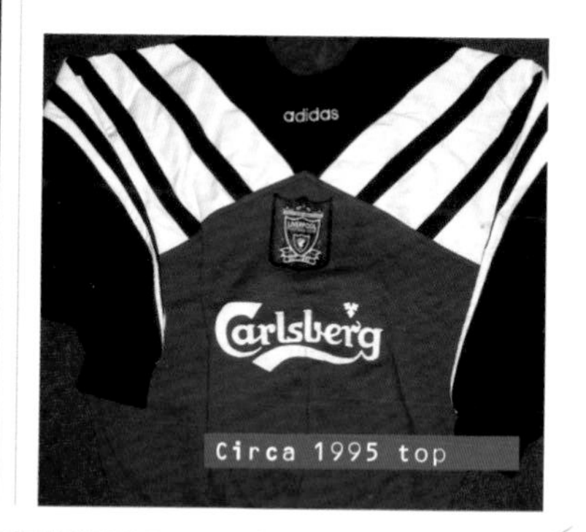

Circa 1995 top

TRAINING TOPS

'Liverpool FC', 90s garb and FA Cup '01

WHAT'S OUR NAME?

Melwood images inextricably linked to the Reds in the early 1970s, these training top variations of Shankly (top) and Toshack (bottom) are captured from the era.

1998-99 - hat unknown

Circa 1992 top

CARDIFF REVISITED

The above fleece was provided to each squad member for the 2001 FA Cup final, although with temperatures touching 30 degrees celsius on the day, it was unlikely to be used!

Mid 1990s coat

THE KIT ADS

Candy and adidas - the late 1980s

CANDY: 1988

Linked in with the club's new sponsorship deal with Italian company Candy (known for their washing machines), Ian Rush had also recently returned from Juventus.

WASHING LINE: 1988-89

This kit advert, reproduced from an original magazine, retained the 'washing' theme - with the main slogan ringing almost true...

TWINS: 1989-91

Although it is unclear whether the duo were actual Liverpool fans, this advert was used to entice fans to the adidas range between 1989-91. Also included in the picture are an LFC bag and club training sweater.

THE KIT ADS

Three kits, one name – adidas

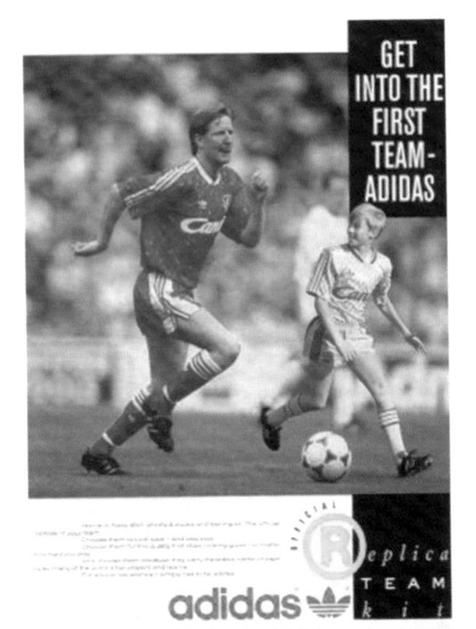

RON AND KID: 1989-91

Another example used to advertise the 1989-91 home and away strips, although Ronnie Whelan appears oblivious to the youngster, seemingly 'stuck on' to the image.

EYES DOWN: 1991-92

The 1991-92 version at least shows how the stars of tomorrow have learnt from the previous ad – to keep their eyes on the football.

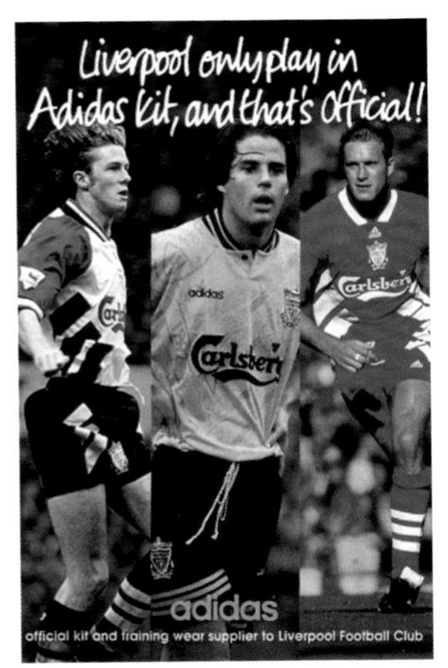

FULL RANGE: 1993-95

All three kits were highlighted in this example, with the yellow strip being sported here by Jamie Redknapp which was only available the following year after being introduced at Sheffield United on Boxing Day 1993.

THE KIT ADS

Yellow kits, Razor's boots and goalie choice

ALTERNATIVE: 1994

Popular demand deemed the release of the third, or 'alternative' kit. Jamie Redknapp was by now a familiar face and was again used to publicise the occasion.

RAZOR: 1995–96

First launched in time for the 1994 World Cup, the adidas Predator boot (designed by former Red Craig Johnston) was claimed to boost the performances of Liverpool defender Neil Ruddock.

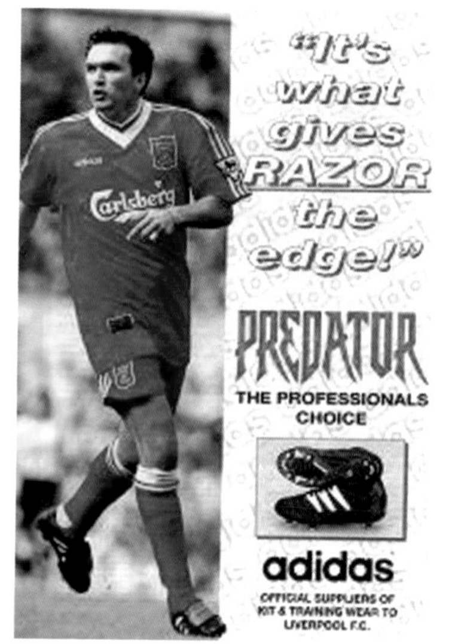

JAMES: 1996

An innovation first brought in at Liverpool during the early days of the first adidas era, two goalkeeper kits had become more common during the 1990s. Although the idea was 'home' and 'away' strips, these would be dependent upon whether the away outfield kit was needed away from Anfield. For example the 'Home James' was worn during the Goodison derby in 1996.

THE KIT ADS

Them there Scousers and a golden touch

BLAME HARRY ENFIELD: 1997–99

Utilising the forever squabbling 'Scousers' from early 1990s comedy staple *Harry Enfield's Television Programme* (which was a parody of Liverpool soap *Brookside*), Reebok decided to launch the new away strip with lookalikes, sitting presumably on the Kop.

GOLD: 2000–02

With the summer launch taking place in an Olympic year (held in Sydney in September/ October 2000), the message could have been used to reflect this. Of course, there was also the small matter of five trophies in 2001!

THE KIT ADS

Cartoon strip and the Royle Family

MARKSMAN: 2001

Goalscoring legend Robbie Fowler is the unfortunate victim in this cartoon to publicise the white away strip for 2001-03. Ironically 'God' would leave for Leeds United by the end of that year.

COUCH POTATOES: 2002

Lifelong Liverpool fan Ricky Tomlinson reprised his Jim Royle role from *The Royle Family* for this 2002-04 home kit advert taken from LFC Magazine. It is not clear whether the character, known for his slobbish ways in the series, influenced the players in any way on or off the pitch!

THE KIT ADS

Abbey Road, away days and a 5-star effort

FAB FOUR: 2004

With heavy leanings towards *The Beatles'* 1969 Abbey Road album cover, the advert was a regular feature of the 2004-06 publicity.

SUMMER DAYS: 2004

Whether or not Michael Owen really did wear his Liverpool shirt on holiday would matter little. By the end of August he would soon be sampling sunnier climes with Real Madrid.

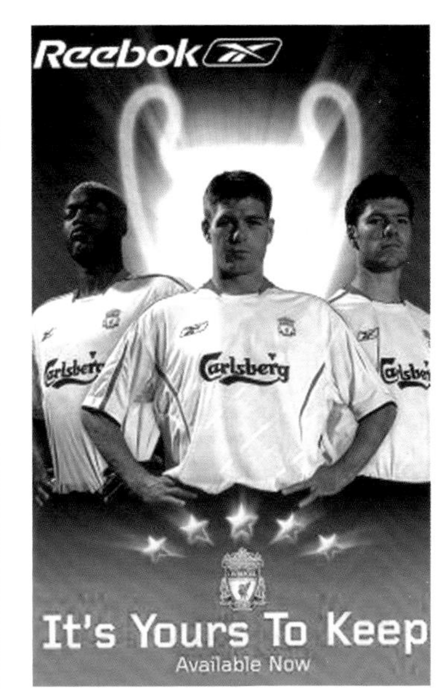

3-STARS?: 2005

Launched on the back of the historic fifth European Cup triumph, Reebok's final away kit was publicised on the back of the news that the club would keep the trophy won in Istanbul. Strangely, only three players were used in the advert.